W9-BVK-776

THE ROCKIES
This first edition belongs to…

_____

Paddlers drift across the glassy surface of Moraine Lake in Canada's Banff National Park.

THE ROCKIES
Pillars of a Continent

BY SCOTT THYBONY • PHOTOGRAPHED BY PAUL CHESLEY

Prepared by the Book Division
National Geographic Society, Washington, D.C.

THE ROCKIES
Pillars of a Continent

By Scott Thybony
Photographed by Paul Chesley

Published by The National Geographic Society
Gilbert M. Grosvenor,
   President and Chairman of the Board
Michela A. English, *Senior Vice President*

Prepared by The Book Division
William R. Gray, *Vice President
   and Director*
Charles Kogod, *Assistant Director*
Barbara A. Payne, *Editorial Director*

Staff for this book
Rebecca Lescaze, *Project Coordinator and
   Senior Researcher*
Margaret Sedeen, *Text Editor*
Charles Kogod, David Ross,
   Illustrations Editors
Suez B. Kehl, *Art Director*
Anne E. Withers, *Researcher*

Carl Mehler, *Map Editor*
Thomas L. Gray, *Map Researcher*
Tibor G. Tóth, *Map Relief*
Martin S. Walz and 3D Geographic
   Technologies, *Map Production*

Lewis R. Bassford,
   Production Project Manager
Richard S. Wain, *Production*

Meredith C. Wilcox, *Illustrations Assistant*
Sandra F. Lotterman, *Editorial Assistant*
Kevin G. Craig, Peggy J. Oxford,
   Staff Assistants

Manufacturing and Quality Management
George V. White, *Director*
John T. Dunn, *Associate Director*
Vincent P. Ryan, *Manager*

Diane L. Coleman, *Indexer*

Copyright © 1996 National Geographic Society. All rights reserved.
Reproduction of the whole or any part of the contents without
written permission is prohibited.

Library of Congress ℭℐℙ Data: page 200

*PRECEDING PAGES: Majestic Grand Teton soars
above northwestern Wyoming in a realm of clouds
and cloud-white snow. Tallest among a cluster of
high crags, the 13,770-foot peak towers over
Jackson Hole, a region wildlife biologist Olaus
Murie called "a country with a spirit."*
*PAGES 4-5: Onlookers in white hats watch a cow-
boy hang tough as a determined bronc tries to buck
him off at a small-town rodeo in Ridgway, Colorado.*

YUKON TERRITORY
NORTHWEST TERRITORIES
Great Slave L. Save
Lake
Athabasca

Liard

+ Terminal
Range
7,750 ft

Fort
Nelson

CANADA
U.S.
ALASKA

CONTINENTAL DIVIDE

Muskwa Ranges

Hart Ranges

BRITISH
COLUMBIA

Peace

Rocky Mountains

G
R
E
A
T

ALBERTA

Athabasca

North Saskatchewan

Columbia Mts.

Fraser
Plateau

Mt Robson
12,972 ft

JASPER
NATIONAL
PARK

Columbia Icefield

YOHO N.P.

Wapta Icefield

BANFF
NATIONAL
PARK

Bow

South Saskatchewan

SASKATCHEWAN

MT. REVELSTOKE N.P.
GLACIER N.P.

KOOTENAY N.P.
The
Bugaboos

CANADA
UNITED STATES

MAN

Fraser

Columbia

Selkirk Mts.

Purcell Mts.

Columbia

GLACIER N.P.
Browning

NORTH
DAKOTA

P

WASHINGTON

Columbia

Bitterroot Range

BOB
MARSHALL
WILDERNESS

Missouri

Big Belt Mts.

MONTANA

Lincoln
Missoula

Yellowstone

SOUTH
DAKOTA

L

Columbia Plateau

Salmon

BIG HOLE NAT. BATTLEFIELD
Lemhi Pass
7,339 ft

Salmon
River
Mountains

YELLOWSTONE
N.P.

Cody

Bighorn Mts.

OREGON

IDAHO

GRAND
TETON N.P.
Jackson

Gannett Peak
13,804 ft

Wind River Range

WYOMING

A

N. Platte

NEBRAS

Snake

South
Pass
7,412 ft

Great Divide
Basin

Sweetwater

Laramie Mts.

Medicine
Bow Mts.

Vedauwoo

N

Steamboat Springs

Longs Peak 14,256 ft

Green

ROCKY MT. N.P.

Denver

Great

Glenwood
Springs

Vail

NEVADA

Basin

UTAH

Aspen

Colorado

Sawatch Ra.

Mt. Elbert 14,433 ft
Pikes Peak 14,110

McClure
Pass
8,755 ft

COLORADO

Arkansas

PACIFIC

Colorado

Ouray
Telluride
Silverton
Durango

San Juan
Mts.

Mt. Eolus
14,084 ft

Sangre de Cristo Mts.

Z

CALIFORNIA

Plateau

Wheeler Peak 13,161 ft

Taos
Chimayo
Santa Fe

+ Point of
Rocks
6,680 ft

OCEAN

ARIZONA

CONTINENTAL DIVIDE

Glorieta
Pass
7,430 ft

NEW MEXICO

Rio Grande

Pecos

0   200 mi
0   400 km

UNITED STATES
MEXICO

TEXAS

FOLLOWING PAGES:

Pages 8–9: Incandescent rays of the setting sun flare above the
southern Rockies near Taos, New Mexico.
Pages 10–11: Quaking aspen sweep up a Colorado mountainside in a blaze of autumn gold.
Pages 12–13: A skier explodes down Telluride Mountain
in a burst of snow and light. Winter draws millions of skiers to the Rockies each year.
Pages 14–15: Steam billows from Yellowstone geysers with the
Teton Range rising in the distance.
Pages 16–17: Sawtooth peaks of the Bugaboos thrust
above Canada's Purcell Mountains. Geologically distinct from ranges to the east
the Purcells draw mountain climbers worldwide.

Southern Ramparts

At Point of Rocks, New Mexico, ranchers Pete and Faye Gaines gaze across the prairie. From this vantage point, many pioneers first saw the distant Rocky Mountains.

*The whole Western world is,
in a sense, but
an expansion of these mountains.*

Walt Whitman

A WINTER SKY arches above the high plains of New Mexico. Layers of blue bend down from the meridian to meet the wide arc of the horizon. Beneath the curve of sky walks rancher Faye Gaines, leading me across the open grasslands. I've come here to the short-grass prairie for a long view of the Rocky Mountains.

Point of Rocks stands to our north. Once a landmark on the Santa Fe Trail, the weathered outcrop gave many travelers their first view of the Rockies. Before us the plains roll upward, taking the eye with them. Only a thick lens of cloud, stretching along the horizon, gives a hint of the mountains to the west. "When clouds lay like that," Faye says, "we know we'll get wind."

A breeze stirs a few strands of her gray hair, cut short, as she talks about the blue grama grass we are crossing. "It's

In traditional dress, Marlena Louise Leno watches dancers in the plaza of Tesuque Pueblo, north of Santa Fe, New Mexico. Pueblo Indians have lived in villages along the Rio Grande since long before the first Europeans arrived there.

a strong grass," Faye says, taking pleasure in one of the essential facts of the land where she has lived all of her life. "It's a miracle grass. You get a little rain, and the next morning you can look out and see a tint of green. The good Lord knew what he was doing when he put that grass here."

As the rise levels off, a line of faraway mountains emerges, so entangled with clouds it's difficult to separate rock from sky. They must be 75 miles away but appear much closer. The vast expanse absorbs all motion; the scene stands as still as a diorama. Thinned by weather and distance, the Rockies appear half formed, a place on the verge of coming into being.

 EARLY TRAVELERS approached the high country with caution. They were leaving behind the known dangers of the Great Plains for the unknown country rising before them. In 1805 Meriwether Lewis recorded his first impressions as he neared the Rockies.

"While I viewed these mountains," he wrote in a journal sprinkled with rough spellings, "I felt a secret pleasure in finding myself so near the head of the heretofore conceived boundless Missouri; but when I reflected on the difficulties which this snowey barrier would most probably throw in my way to the Pacific, and the sufferings and hardships of myself and party in thim, it in some measure counterballanced the joy I had felt in the first moments in which I gazed on them."

In the years following the Lewis and Clark expedition, those traveling by wagon avoided the higher elevations. Wagon trains followed either the Oregon Trail through Wyoming's South Pass, the main break in the mountain front, or skirted the Rockies by way of the Santa Fe Trail.

Pausing a moment, Faye and I look across a wide swale to a remnant of the legendary trail that linked Missouri with Santa Fe. Faint wagon ruts, shallow and grass-covered, score the shoulder of the opposite ridge. The tracks waver slightly over the uneven ground the way a raindrop might slide down a windowpane. The multiple ruts, Faye mentions, show how the freight caravans spread out when on the move. "They didn't go single file the way you see in the movies. Why would you travel like that and eat someone's dirt all the way?"

Rock piles, scattered about us, mark the graves of unknown travelers who were buried where they died. Nearby lies a circle, about 12 feet in diameter, of flat stones used to anchor a tepee cover. As we continue, more tepee rings appear on the site of an old Plains Indian camp. Apache, Comanche, and other nomadic tribes once crossed this region to trade, hunt buffalo, and raid. A reliable spring, next to high ground, drew them to this camp for generations. "They could sit up there on the point," the rancher says, "and see for days."

Ahead, Faye's family waits in the pickup to take us up Point of Rocks. She climbs in back with her granddaughter, and I scoot next to her husband, Pete, who wears a canvas jacket over a pair of suspenders. With their son, Gary, behind the wheel, we bounce up a rocky track, talking about the condition of the range. Some of the springs on the ranch are drying up from drought, Pete tells me. "We'll have to turn them over to the rattlesnakes and the horny toads again."

Reaching the rim, Gary swings the truck around to face west. The far mountains hang on the skyline, gathering snow clouds as they float above the dry grasslands. Even at this distance the Rockies have an unmistakable presence.

We sit for a moment and look at the Sangre de Cristo range spreading out before us, where the southern Rockies meet the plains. Far to the south lies Glorieta Pass, a notch in the mountain front. Flanked by tablelands on one side and mountains on the other, the pass marks the end of the mesa country and the beginning of the Rockies.

That's Baldy on the north," Pete says, trying to sort the uplands from the clouds, "then Touch Me Not and Wheeler, the tallest peak in New Mexico."

To get a sense of the whole, I've come here to the open plains. But the mountains before us span the horizon from one end to the other. What I can see is only a part of something much larger. The Sangre de Cristos are one of at least 50 distinct ranges contained within the Rocky Mountain system. And the Rockies themselves form only the easternmost chain of the immense North American Cordillera running from Mexico into Alaska.

Some geographers take it even farther, linking the ranges of North America with the cordillera of South America in an intercontinental system. The "back-bone of our hemisphere" poet Walt Whitman called the cordillera on a tour of the Colorado Rockies in 1879. "The whole Western world is, in a sense," he wrote, "but an expansion of these mountains."

Beginning here in northern New Mexico, the Rockies traverse the western United States. They continue deep into Canada and merge with the plateau country of northern British Columbia. Geographers differ on how far to extend the Rockies. Some include ranges to the north; some add those farther south. But the main chain stretches for almost 2,000 straight-line miles across country where a straight mile, unless measured on a flat map, is hard to find.

Not only do the Rockies meander, they lift and subside and lift again in a succession of ridges and peaks. Geologists trace their origin to a period of mountain building known as the Laramide Orogeny. This tectonic event began about a hundred million years ago and continued for millions of years. Uplift in some parts of the range is still occurring. Created by continental forces deep within the earth, the Rockies have been shaped locally by the grind of ice and the cutting flow of meltwater.

Thrust from the plains, already a mile above the sea, the mountain mass rises another vertical mile with dozens of peaks cresting two-thirds of a mile higher. Along the spine of the Rockies lie the headwaters of many of the great western rivers, fed by snowmelt and runoff. The Mackenzie and the Columbia, the Missouri and the Arkansas, the Colorado and the Rio Grande all begin on the Continental Divide. From this line of separation, waters flowing east to the Atlantic Ocean and north into the Arctic part from those draining west into the Pacific. But the same mountains that divide the waters also bind the region together. Spanning 25 degrees of latitude and a range of ecosystems and cultural traditions, the Rockies retain an essential unity, a cohesiveness.

Earlier in the fall, I had returned to the Rocky Mountains after an absence of nearly a decade. I was beginning a journey, to be taken in stages, along the length of the range. As soon as I entered the high country, the sense of place

The once powerful Pecos Pueblo now lies in ruins at the foot of of the Rockies, but in 1540 the shrill whistle of bone flutes greeted the arrival of Spanish soldiers here.

returned. The recognition came from the mountain air itself, sharpened by the scent of evergreens and the volatile swings of weather. And it came from the massive scale of the surroundings, the perception of space expanding beyond the limits.

In the months to come, I will travel into the heart of the Rockies, wherever it may lie. Some say it's the Tetons, others claim the high peaks of Colorado or the northern ranges of Canada. Sometimes I'll go alone, but more often with those who know the mountains and have come to terms with them—the rangers and scientists, the buckaroos, cragsmen, and geyser gazers. With no set route to follow, I'll begin with the mountains of northern New Mexico where the human presence remains deeply rooted. Generations of Pueblo Indians and the descendants of Spanish colonists have made the Sangre de Cristo Mountains their home, giving the southernmost Rockies a distinct character.

Leaving Pete's pickup, I walk to the end of the point where the land drops away into the wide open. The vast distances absorb the details of the terrain, letting the primary lines emerge. Yellow plains spread westward to the foot of the mountains where the surface tilts into blue slopes. Somewhere above lie the summits, blanketed by snow and cloud-hidden. As I stand there, a rift suddenly opens and sunlight floods across a high snowfield.

An eagle dancer swoops before drummers in Tesuque Pueblo. In the southern Rockies, Spanish and Pueblo Indian traditions blend, giving the region its distinctive character.

Faye walks over. "Isn't it magnificent?" she asks. No answer is needed. Before us, the great mountains of the West rise, pushing the horizon far above the plains. The highest peaks have disappeared into a landscape of the imagination.

*L*EAVING POINT OF ROCKS, I cross the mountains to Taos. The sound of drumming pulses through the winter air, coming from the mountain side of Taos Pueblo. A small crowd has gathered before an adobe church in northern New Mexico, waiting in the cold for the buffalo dancers to appear. Yesterday's snowstorm has tapered off in time for the ceremony to begin.

Pueblo Indian women huddle together, wrapped in colorful shawls held tightly against the wind. Stripes of reds, yellows, and blues run vertically down their backs. Behind them presses a line of visitors with heads turned toward the stir of movement across the plaza.

Shreds of chanting, carried by the wind, reach the onlookers. On a wall above them stands a Taos boy, watching. "The buffalo dancers!" he shouts. His lack of restraint draws a sharp look from a woman wearing high deerskin moccasins. "The buffalo dancers," he repeats. "They're coming!"

Village leaders cross the wide plaza at the head of a procession. Behind them, terraced rooftops step upward against a backdrop of cloud-buried ridges. The men, wrapped in blankets and with faces painted red, carry brass-knobbed canes of office. Some of the leaders wear their hair in long braids. A chorus of singers follows, each beating a hand drum. As the vanguard nears the church they veer to one side to let the herd of almost 50 buffalo dancers surge forward. The women greet them, crying out in a high tremolo, piercing and unexpected.

Under enormous shaggy heads with curving black horns, the dancers begin. Feet move in place, pounding the snow-packed ground with ponderous steps repeated again and again. The kilted dancers have covered their bare chests with only a wash of red paint. Each holds a single arrow; each buffalo head is topped by an eagle feather. An archaic mood, solemn and ritualistic, settles over the pueblo as the Indians join in a winter dance beneath their sacred mountain.

Antlers of an elk and several mule deer branch upward in sharp tines above the throng. Holding sticks as forelegs, the deer dancers stand motionless while the buffalo churn about them. Hides hang loose and fleshy down their backs; a red tongue dangles from a deer head. Watching from the side, I suddenly realize these are not costumes but fresh kills.

The hunters are dancing in the skins of their prey.

A visitor climbs onto a snowbank and looks below at the mass of animal dancers moving to the drumbeats. "Holy smokes!" he says with a Texas accent. "This is intense. I've never seen anything like it."

Traditionally, the Taos Indians relied on hunting more than other Pueblo tribes did. Each year they crossed the Sangre de Cristo Mountains and entered the plains to chase the buffalo. Their pack trail joined the Santa Fe Trail near Point of Rocks. After the buffalo disappeared, the Taos Indians continued their annual trek, hunting the antelope and prairie elk that remained. Ranchers remember seeing Pueblo families stringing across the plains on their last hunt early this century.

Taos Indians and their ancestors have lived at the foot of the mountains, in their present village, for six centuries. The first Europeans passed through in 1540 with the Coronado expedition, followed by Spanish colonists who settled on the outskirts of the Indian pueblo. Three centuries after Coronado, American traders and fur trappers arrived on the scene.

From throughout the southern Rockies, mountain men converged on Taos to sell their beaver pelts. Before returning to the higher elevations, they sampled the local whiskey, called Taos Lightning, and cut loose at a fandango or two.

Some of the trappers, Kit Carson among them, ended up staying as the fur trade diminished. The Carson home, now a museum, sits off the town plaza in Taos, pressed between gift

At San Ildefonso Pueblo, Diane Calabaza bakes bread with the help of her niece, Stacie Solomon. Pueblo women fire up hornos—*beehive-shaped ovens—to prepare food for their guests on the day of a ceremonial dance.*

FOLLOWING PAGES: Cliffs swallow the Rio Grande as it flows through a deep gorge. The Sangre de Cristo Mountains, in the distance, flank the broad valley.

shops and galleries. On the walls of a back room hang old Chimayo weavings with patterns as bold as the range of mountains above town.

Wheeler Peak, the highest summit in the state at 13,161 feet, dominates the valley. On its slopes lies Blue Lake, returned to the Taos people in 1970 after more than half a century of political struggle. From Blue Lake flows the river that sustains those living in the village below. Each year members of the pueblo retrace the river to its source, following a trail known as the "path of life." Their pilgrimage ends high in the mountains on the edge of the lake called by a Taos leader "a place of prayer for all life."

The procession completes the first round of dancing and moves to the foot of the multistoried north house. Walls of sun-dried brick stack upward in receding tiers five stories high. Outside ladders reach the upper floors. The blues and greens of painted doors perforate a few of the mud-brown room blocks where coats of adobe stucco soften the stark lines of wall and roof.

Remains of an outer defensive wall enclose the old pueblo. Once meant to deflect attacks by mounted raiders, the barrier now guards against threats to the traditional way of life. When Taos became the last Indian pueblo to allow electricity, the people insisted that the buried lines end 250 feet from the wall to keep the integrity of the old village intact.

At the conclusion of the second set, the animals shift to the next location and take up the dance again. Snow, shoveled from the dance ground, lies humped next to a beehive-shaped oven. Onlookers crowd together as the buffalo resume their dancing.

Standing with them I watch the animals sway left and right and back again, the motion repeated hypnotically. In the biting cold, I listen to the steady tread of feet moving to the rhythmic chanting. My thoughts begin to drift off, lulled by the repetitions of movement and chant. But suddenly the pieces of the ceremony fall into place.

Voices of the singers drop into another range, entering a fuller dimension of sound. Colors deepen. On the rooftop above, a Pueblo mother stands apart from the other women, silhouetted against the sky. She wears a red shawl wrapped around both herself and a child, a streak of brilliance against the storm-gray clouds.

I look around to see if anyone else has noticed the shift, but expressions remain unchanged and the dance goes on. Within a few minutes the sounds flatten again, and the colors fade back to normal.

The procession divides before the last round begins. One

group crosses the river to the south house; the other remains on the north side. The final dancing takes place next to kivas where long, tapered ladders leave the underground chambers and reach far into the sky. For a moment, sunlight streams through the clouds and falls on the backs of the dancers.

As the ceremony ends, the crowd trickles away. Buffalo dancers withdraw to the kiva roofs and straighten up, appearing to return to their human forms. Behind them rise the mountains, a vertical mass dissolving into the clouds.

*B*Y NEXT MORNING the storm has blown past. Above Taos, the gleaming white of the main peak cuts deep into the blue. I join my friends Maria Teresa García and Marc Thompson, both archaeologists, on a drive to Picuris Pueblo.

Following a two-lane blacktop, we cross a spur ridge and drop into a hidden valley. The houses of Picuris, the highest of the pueblos and home to about 275 people, lie clustered on the mountainside.

As we stroll through the sunlit community, a voice calls out from the hill above. Richard Mermejo, a tribal leader, invites us up to the oldest quarter of the pueblo. Wearing a winter cap with long earflaps, a graying goatee, and dark sunglasses, he escorts us into the plaza. The men have been shoveling snow from the roof of the Sky kiva to

Ristras—garlands—of red chiles hang outside the door at the Taos home of the legendary mountain man, Kit Carson. Inside, a visitor's shadow falls across a portrait of Carson.

prepare for an upcoming ceremony. Room blocks of weathered adobe face each other across the open space.

"Those rooms," Richard says, "were here when Gaspar Castaño de Sosa came to the valley in 1591. This was the last pueblo the Spanish found. Even from the highest peak, you can't see the old village. It was hidden."

Early Spanish accounts described Picuris as one of the largest terraced pueblos in the region, but where it stood isn't apparent. I ask if this was the location of the original pueblo.

"It's still here," Marc says, his hair tightly braided in a queue. "This mound isn't natural. It's right beneath your feet. The rooms are still here, buried."

Smoke rolls up from the ground-level hatchway as a fire warms the subterranean chamber. Richard looks across the plaza where kiva poles angle skyward above a spur of the southern Rockies. "This place," he says with deep feeling, "is the center of our world."

After saying goodbye to my friends, I head south toward Santa Fe. The high road strings together villages still grounded in their Spanish heritage. Reaching Chimayo, I pull into a weaving shop run by the Trujillo family.

Seven generations of the family have used their treadle looms to make colorful blankets, in a weaving tradition followed by many of the local families. Inside the shop, weavings cover the walls. Horizontal stripes run across a Chimayo-style blanket, the central designs reflecting both Hispanic and Indian elements. Skeins of wool hang in the back room—blues, reds, and a pale yellow dyed from the flower of the *chamiso*—rabbitbrush—a plant found scattered across the arroyos.

CONTINUING THROUGH the narrow streets of the old village, I pass ristras of red chiles hanging from doorways. Sweet piñon smoke scents the air as I cross the grounds of the Santuario de Chimayo. Between the twin towers of the church, melting snow drips down the adobe walls in dark streaks. Each year El Santuario draws thousands of Catholic pilgrims during Holy Week. The faithful come on foot from throughout northern New Mexico, some walking for days to reach the healing shrine.

As I enter the dim interior of the church, waxy smoke from votive candles floats in the air. No one else is around. I walk down the nave, past carved wooden pews, to the altar. Behind it rises an elaborately painted *retablo*, or altarpiece. Stripes of blues and reds fill panels of the altar screen, as crowded with color and motion as the local weavings. Suspended above the altar is a crucifix. Blood streams from the wounds of the Corpus, a fitting image for a church in the foothills of the Sangre de Cristos, mountains named for the blood of Christ.

Ducking through a low doorway, I reach a back chamber. From a hole in the earthen floor, the devout gather handfuls of dirt that bears a reputation for miraculous cures. Crutches hang from walls together with testimonials attesting to the curative power of the shrine. On impulse I take a pinch of dirt and stick it in my pocket unsure of what I'll do with it. I retrace my steps through the church.

A man in a beret stands among the gravestones outside, gazing up at the near hills. A retired priest who continues to serve the church as associate pastor, he tells me his name is Father Casimire Roca. Father Roca arrived in New Mexico 40 years ago when the mountain roads were still unpaved and before telephone lines had reached these remote valleys.

"Most of those who come here are Hispanic," he says, "but sometimes Indians also visit. When they do, entire families arrive together. Each of them carries a candle when they enter the church to pray. I honor them," the pastor adds. "They are very devout."

The priest turns to go and looks up. Clumps of juniper dot the surrounding foothills. "I love these mountains," he says with a smile.

Crutches line the wall of a chapel (opposite) as testimony to cures received by the faithful. Ten-year-old Angelica Domínguez comes to pray every day at the shrine of El Santuriaro de Chimayo in the mountain foothills.

FOLLOWING PAGES: Visitors shop for Indian crafts outside Santa Fe's Palace of the Governors. The oldest capitol building in the United States, it was built by Spanish settlers in 1606-10.

*Morning light strikes
the adobe walls of
San Gerónimo de
Taos (right), where
Mike Concha (above),
governor of Taos
Pueblo, stands before
the church.*

*PRECEDING PAGES:
The Sangre de Cristo
Mountains—a
Rockies range—
spread from central
Colorado to northern
New Mexico. Swiss
psychiatrist Carl
Jung called them
"the roof of the
American continent."*

Below the rugged slopes of the southern Rocky Mountains, ristras, pottery, bright-hued rugs, and festive Mexican serapes cover the wall of a gift shop near Taos.

FOLLOWING PAGES: Bleached skulls, often a painting subject for artist Georgia O'Keeffe, decorate galleries and homes in the Southwest.

Heart of the Rockies

Tall evergreen spires rise from the Face of Bell on Aspen Mountain, deep in the Colorado Rockies. Nearly lost in the expanse of snow and trees, skiers descend the mogul-carved slope.

This is a beautiful world and all who go out under the open sky will feel the gentle influences of nature.

Enos A. Mills

SEVERAL FORERUNNERS ski past, putting the final touches on the downhill course. A moment later the first racer appears on the slope above. He is moving fast and quietly as the mountainside drops from beneath his skis. For an instant the downhill racer flies above the angle of the slope until his skis reconnect with the snow-covered ground. Moving at an unreal speed, he leans into the steep turn and disappears down the mountain.

Crowds have been gathering all morning at the foot of Aspen Mountain in the heart of the Colorado Rockies. Camera and radio crews have staked out positions overlooking the finish line, ready for action if the weather cooperates. Yesterday, the men's downhill never took place. The World Cup ski race was snowed out.

Mention the Rockies and many people think snow—

High above Aspen, Colorado, a ski racer makes final adjustments at the top of the course. In a moment, she will fly down the slope at speeds as high as 70 miles an hour. Each year the mountain town draws the world's top skiers to compete in World Cup events.

47

deep, Rocky Mountain powder. Despite travel conditions, millions of people converge on Colorado's ski slopes each winter. I've joined the influx, to watch the world's best skiers compete in America's Downhill. Taking the advice of a friend, I kick-step up an ungroomed slope to a wide turn in the run. I join a cluster of race officials and ski patrollers gathered where the course detours around a tree island.

From the starting gate to the finish line, the downhill course covers a distance of 3,050 feet. Net fencing, designed to absorb the impact of a skier moving at 80 miles an hour, lines the slopes. Top racers take less than a minute and 45 seconds to ski the course, while dropping more than 2,500 vertical feet. Fractions of a second determine the outcome.

Soon the next downhill racer zips past and others follow at one-minute intervals. As they pass by, the only sounds are the hiss and rasp of skis skimming the snow. They wear bright yellows and skintight reds, the team colors of France, Austria, Norway, Italy, and other competing countries. Suddenly a racer takes the turn too wide and almost falls. "Oo-la-la," says a judge in a rare comment.

A TV cameraman, perched on a platform above, tracks movement high on the ski run. Unable to see the top of the course from my position, I know American downhiller AJ—no periods—Kitt, the local favorite, is on the move by the cheers following him down the mountain. Soon I see him, slicing in an aerodynamic tuck, cutting a smooth trajectory. No holding back, no hesitation. "He's pushing it," shouts a ski patroller.

AJ enters a straightaway, weaving through speed-control gates and dropping swiftly down the mountain. Just above the curve, he lifts into the air and hangs suspended for an instant. Suddenly he's down and into the turn, hitting just the right line as he carves an arc of pure speed. A flash of blue lycra and he's gone. A moment later cheers erupt from the spectators crowding the finish line below. A voice comes over a two-way radio saying that AJ has taken the lead.

But the weather continues to deteriorate. Trees stand snow-frosted. After a few more runs, officials halt the race until conditions improve. Heavy snow continues to fall, obscuring the streets and brick buildings filling the valley.

After a 12-minute delay, the forerunners again ski the course, signaling a resumption of the race. Norwegian skier Asgeir Linberg sweeps into view. He leans into the tight curve, almost brushing the slope as he fights the centrifugal forces pulling outward. He pushes to the limit and then a little more. Coming out of the curve too wide, Linberg loses control. Instantly he crashes in a whirl of poles and skis and flying snow. He plows through the first safety fence below me and flattens the second. I hear a sharp cry and know he's injured.

Slogging knee-deep through powder, I reach Linberg. He is sitting up, stunned. The snow about him is splattered with blood, the red bright on the white. Blood stains the mound of snow he has packed around the fracture of his left arm. Blood trickles from his nose. A ski patroller reaching the scene quickly checks his vital signs and asks about other injuries. In pain, the skier answers with difficulty. Falling snow melts on his back, and I throw my parka over his shoulders.

As I support Linberg's arm, the ski patroller wraps a splint around it. The rest of the team arrives with a toboggan to take him off the mountain to an ambulance. Snowflakes continue to drift through the air. A course official looks into the gray sky.

The race is canceled. Wind sweeps the course as a couple in matching fur coats and cowboy hats scurry toward the shelter of the Hard Rock Cafe tent. They steer clear of two fans wearing horned helmets and shouting in Norwegian.

Entering the line of traffic leaving Aspen, I take the highway along the Roaring Fork River. A stretch limo with a ski rack on top heads the other way, back to the slopes. Clouds of steam billow up from the open-air spa when I reach Glenwood Springs. A few inveterate soakers relax in the hot pools, oblivious to the falling snow.

Anxious to cross the mountains before the storm closes the high passes, I head east on Interstate 70. The highway links the western canyons with the plains, traversing one of the highest sections of the Rocky Mountains. Beyond town, the road follows the Colorado River in sweeping curves.

Traffic moves smoothly until the ski runs above Vail come into view. Cars and trucks quickly close to a standstill, packed together as solidly as a snowslide. Vail Pass is closed. I turn off the engine and wait. Listening to the radio, I learn that avalanches have closed the roads leading to Silverton in the San Juans, isolating the mountain town.

A FEW MONTHS BEFORE, I had begun my journey into the Rocky Mountains with a trip to the San Juans, hurrying into the high country before the autumn colors peaked. Walking down a back street of Durango, I could sense the closeness of the mountains. They began just beyond the brick walls of the old mining town, a great mass of ice-scarred ranges pushing north with no hint of where they might end. Carrying a backpack, I turned a corner toward the train station.

"Bo—ooard!" shouted a conductor in a voice pitched to carry the length of the train. A whistle pierced the air as steam geysered straight into the morning sky. The passengers surged

across the platform to take their seats. I joined the scramble on board for the ride into the San Juan Mountains.

With a lurch, the engine left the station, pulling a string of yellow cars. It chugged through town, following the tracks of the Durango & Silverton Narrow Gauge Railroad, completed in 1882. The rocky debris of a terminal moraine lay on the outskirts of town, marking the farthest advance of a glacier at the end of the Ice Age. In the valley above, humps of bedrock shouldered above the fields, rounded by the drag of ice.

Although the glacier had retreated long ago, the abrupt change of weather made it feel like the cold had never left. I stared out the window as the train swayed and swung along the Animas River through pasturelands sparkling with frost.

Under a winter-storm warning, the train headed toward a gap in the southwestern wall of the Rockies. Snow-laden clouds hung overhead, sagging in dark folds. Thickets of Gambel oak blanketed the mountainsides in a patchwork of soft yellows and reds. A grove of green-leafed aspens crowded one ravine and another stand burned golden yellow in the

People at Steamboat Springs come to terms with winter by turning it into a festival. At night the snowy slopes flare up with torch-carrying skiers (left) and the "Lighted Man," Jon Banks (opposite).

FOLLOWING PAGES: Golden foliage lingers in a high-country grove south of Aspen, as a dusting of snow signals the approach of winter.

next. Near the tracks, cottonwood and box elder screened the riverbanks with foliage just beginning to change.

Climbing steadily, the train entered a gorge leading into the high country. After an initial flurry of clicking and whirring cameras, the sightseers had settled into their seats. Strangers talked across the aisle in the open manner of people who would never meet again.

Smoke curled from the stack as the train looped back upon itself, hugging the canyon wall high above the Animas. The wood-paneled cars shuddered and clanked as I left my seat and joined the brakeman, Barney Bunker, on the platform outside.

"They call this the High Line," he said, looking down a sheer cliff to the river 400 feet below. A narrow shelf had been blasted into the rock wall to hold the tracks. Dark spires of spruce and fir grew from the ledges and crevices below where bottle-green water broke into white cascades. The river funneled through a cut in the 1.78-billion-year-old Twilight gneiss, the oldest rock in the San Juans.

Three hours after leaving Durango, the train pulled into Needle Park. In summer, more than a hundred backpackers might disembark here on a busy day. But on this fall day I was the only one. As I grabbed my pack, the brakeman instructed me on how to flag down the train on my return. "Don't wave your arms above your head," he said. "It looks like you're trying to be friendly. We'll just wave back and keep on going. Move your arms back and forth across the knees. Do the Charleston."

On the far side of the river, forested slopes angled sharply upward to end in sawtooth peaks a mile higher than the train. Aspen clustered in bright constellations of yellow against the night-green conifers. The mountain air had a bite to it as I crossed the footbridge over the Animas.

Feeling the cold, I increased my pace to warm up. The trail entered the forest, passing a couple of cabins already boarded up for the season. One by one, squirrels erupted in

warning chatters, triggered like motion sensors by my approach. Aspen leaves carpeted the pathway in pointillist dabs of yellow.

A couple of miles farther, sunlight broke through the clouds and struck the far slope, falling among the quaking aspen. With the shift of seasons, the fading green had allowed the underlying pigments to burn through in a release of chromatic energy. The mountain came alive with the vibratory yellow of shimmering leaves.

Continuing up the footpath of decomposed granite, I walked through stands of tall conifers. Spruce and fir, flanking the trail, began to dominate the mix of trees. Wispy strands of lichen, Old Man's Beard, hung from the branches in a green so pale as to appear gray. Screened from view, the creek plunged below in a rush and rumble of white noise.

On top of the next ridge I reached the snow cover. Last night's storm had dusted tree boughs and dropped a few inches on the ground where it lay fresh and untracked. As I entered the lower end of Chicago Basin, the trees gave way to a sunny alpine meadow, circled by conifer spires and topped by a skyline of jagged crags. The bend of the canyon hid the full view of the highest summits until the last moment. Everything stood on end. Trees grew as straight as flagpoles, pointing toward sharp-cut peaks that climbed much higher.

Reaching a grove of Englemann spruce, I dropped my pack and made camp near timberline. A few hundred feet higher, standing trees gave way to the ground-huggers. As I pitched a tent, snow fell so lightly it settled to the ground like wisps of cloud. The weather was taking a turn toward winter.

On the map I counted nine peaks enclosing a basin formed by compound cirques at the headwaters of the creek. Storm clouds from the west surged over the lower ridges, bumping into the highest summits—Eolus, Sunlight, and Windom—all reaching above 14,000 feet in elevation.

A NUMBER OF YEARS AGO I was returning with a group from the summit of Windom. We'd decided to cross the intervening valley and climb Sunlight Peak before returning to camp. It was a calculated risk. Storms, moving in from three directions, looked as if they would converge overhead within an hour or two. We descended a snowfield, using ice axes to glissade down the slope, and pushed hard up the far ridge toward Sunlight. Nearing the top, I felt the skin on my face begin to prickle. Checking the back of my hands, I saw the fine hairs standing up. The air had become electrically charged. I ignored the warning, thinking we still had time to reach the summit.

Dark clouds churned above as we continued to scramble up the rocks. We were within a hundred feet of the top when lightning exploded in a tremendous crash of blinding light. Ducking into a crouch, I waited for the next strike as thunder rolled between the ridges. We lost all interest in reaching the top. Totally exposed, our group began a fast descent with lightning striking above and below us. Once on the valley floor we spread out and squatted low to reduce the odds of getting hit. Strikes came in quick succession, the thunder was continuous, rolling down from the heights and echoing deep and solemn off the ridges. When the heaviest discharge had eased somewhat, we descended to camp without talking, driven inside our own thoughts by the enormity of the storm.

Now, putting away the map, I turned in with a plan to hike to a pair of high lakes in the morning. At first light, I took a day pack and headed toward the serrated crest above. I had come to the mountains to catch the fall season but now left it behind, drawn into the early winter of the high peaks.

Creeks slid down the slopes, their flow reduced to a trickle by the night's freeze-up. Water slipped from ledge to ancient ledge, spilling across the Eolus granite, almost 1.5 billion years old. An hour after sunrise, a light snow began to fall.

Leaving the trail, I noticed pale yellow tailings angling down from an old mine shaft. Vegetation had yet to take root on the spoil pile a century after it had been worked. In the late 1870s, prospectors had combed the granite outcrops of Chicago Basin. Limited silver mining continued through the turn of the 20th century.

Above the timber, I climbed steadily higher, dodging clumps of ground-hugging willow. In the higher elevations even the surfaces of the streams were frozen. My plan was to go only as far as Twin Lakes, a pair of glacial tarns, but I found myself veering off toward Mount Eolus, at 14,084 feet, one of the local "fourteeners." I'd climbed it before, and now couldn't resist taking a closer look.

As I stopped to adjust my gear, a yellow-bellied marmot warned its companions of my presence with a chirping bark. Bare crags rimmed the horizon. These ragged summits had remained above the level of the glaciers during the Pleistocene, as granite islands in an expanse of slow-moving ice. Lacking an ice ax and mittens, I wasn't prepared for a climb. But I covered my hands with an extra pair of socks and pushed on.

The route I was following led to the ridgeline up an inclined snowfield. As the slope steepened, I was forced to kick-step my way up. The higher I went, the more acute the angle became. Near the top, the snow slope narrowed into a steep, exposed chute. I could easily lose my footing if the snow conditions changed and take a long slide back down to autumn. After a long look, I backed off, retraced my steps, and returned to camp under a lowering sky.

That night I woke up to a high-pitched, nose-in-the-air howl. The cry of the coyote sounded so lost and forlorn it bypassed my ears, slivering its way beneath my skin. Hours later I again rolled awake to a call far out in the night.

An eerie whistling came from beyond the grove where I had camped. Disoriented at first, I took a moment to remember where I was and to recognize the drawn-out bugling of a bull elk. Another answered in the distance with a low-pitched call that leaped up to a screeching whistle. The note was held long and high until it tumbled off into empty silence at last.

*A*FTER A TWO-HOUR WAIT below Vail Pass, traffic on I-70 begins to crawl up the mountain. Stranded vehicles litter the roadsides and a moving van lies jackknifed in the middle of the highway. Frustrated by the long delays, cars careen up the switchbacks to try to make up for lost time. A frenzy takes over this winter crossing of the mountains as daylight fails and the highway climbs and descends through air dense with falling snow. Somewhere to the south rises Mount Elbert, at 14,433 feet the highest summit in the Rocky Mountains.

Colorado contains within its boundaries more than 50

Weekend miners, on a slope above Aspen, take a break from working their claim. Mining played a key role in the settlement of the Rockies and in shaping the character of mountain towns.

peaks rising above 14,000 feet. The San Juan Mountains are the most extensive range, the Sawatch the highest, and the Front Range, with its proximity to major urban areas, the most visited. It stretches from Pikes Peak in the south to Longs Peak in the north, with branches trailing into Wyoming.

Next day, on my way to Rocky Mountain National Park, I pull off the road and unload the skis. Snow drifts dust-fine through a patch of sunlight, along the shore of Brainard Lake.

Reaching a break in the trees, I spot a man sitting hunched over with his back to the wind, holding a fishing pole. As I cross the lake ice to join him, the wind blows me sideways. Ice fisherman Brad Jensen sits on an upturned bucket, watching his two lines dangle through holes he's cut in the ice. He wears layers of pile clothing beneath thick canvas coveralls.

"How many fish have you caught?" I ask.

"Fish and Game says a fisherman is doing well to catch one an hour," he tells me. "I've caught 65 this morning." The bobber dips as he's talking and he pulls in number 66. Scales flash as the trout flicks back and forth on the line. "It's a brookie."

"You said you've caught 65 fish today?" I ask to make sure I heard him clearly. He corrects me—it's 66. A minute later he reels in a rainbow trout, number 67. Eight trout, the only ones he's keeping, lie frozen stiff in the sled.

I ski back to the road and head north to meet the daughter of Enos A. Mills, legendary guide and self-taught naturalist. His passion for saving wild country led to the creation of Rocky Mountain National Park.

Clouds hide the face of Longs Peak, high above, as the cold air settles around us. Enda Mills Kiley, in her mid-70s, is dressed for the weather, with her long winter coat and a purple stocking cap. Using a ski pole as a walking stick, she leads me down the path to the cabin built by her father in 1885.

"He somehow sensed how nature fits," she says, "how all the pieces fit together. He was urging people everywhere to save a place, to preserve a park. He said a park is a refuge, an island of safety in a riotous world."

When he lived in the one-room cabin, bookshelves lined the walls. A simple table filled one corner and a bed, next to a woodstove, took up another. These spare furnishings provided plenty of comfort for a man who often climbed alone into the mountains without a tent or sleeping bag. Bear-paw snowshoes still hang from the rafters, a reminder of the epic treks Enos made as a snow observer for the state of Colorado. One winter he snowshoed down the Continental Divide from Wyoming to New Mexico, measuring the snowpack along the way.

I study the black-and-white pictures on the walls. One shows the lean and weathered mountaineer standing on a peak.

Spring arrives in Aspen, marked by an annual ski picnic. Colorful costumes add to

the festivities as revelers dance on the snow in fur coats and ski boots.

Another finds him holding the hand of a little girl. "That's me," Enda says.

Enos Mills' 15 books and numerous magazine articles recount a lifetime of adventures—riding an avalanche on snowshoes, finding his way out of the mountains while snow-blind, studies of beavers and grizzly bears.

Over the years, Mills witnessed the impact people were having on the mountains. "Every year he noticed there were two or three fewer grizzly bears than he'd seen the year before," his daughter says. "He knew that sooner or later the bears he was watching would disappear. There was a mother bear he tried to save, but someone had gone to her den and killed her, leaving the little ones. That one instance, as much as any other, influenced his idea of a park.

"From 1909 to 1915 he gave his life to speaking in favor of the Front Range as a national park," Enda says. The campaign to set aside areas of great natural beauty gained momentum through his lectures and writings. In 1915, Rocky Mountain National Park became a reality.

On the cabin wall hangs a plaque quoting Enos Mills: "This is a beautiful world and all who go out under the open sky will feel the gentle influences of nature." I mention my hope for some gentle weather tomorrow when I will head into the mountains with the Longs Peak ranger. "There's no such thing as bad weather," Enda tells me. "My father said it just added to the experience."Early next morning, park ranger Jim Detterline is working his climbing boot over an air cast. He had taken a fall last week, injuring his ankle, but he's determined not to let that slow him down. Last night he went dancing to limber up for today's climb, a tradition he didn't want to break despite his injury. "I'm ready," he tells me.

T'S STILL DARK OUTSIDE the guide's cabin below Longs Peak in Rocky Mountain National Park. Jim lives here with his turtles and snakes, reminders of what he calls his "reptile days." He has a Ph.D. in biology and a passion for mountains.

Crutches lean against the wall next to his mountaineering skis. A collection of well-used ice axes hangs on the door. We're taking climbing gear with us—ice axes and crampons, ropes and helmets—in case the weather gives us a chance to go for the summit. We've kept our plans simple: head into the mountains and see what happens. In his late 30s with a blonde mustache and darker beard, Detterline has been the Longs Peak climbing ranger for ten years. He has conducted more than 500 search-and-rescues. His interest in mountain rescue began after he'd been trapped by a storm on the North Face of

Grand Teton. He hung from the 2,500-foot cliff for six nights before his rescue. "It amazed me," he says, "that somebody'd put their life on the line for somebody they didn't know."

Lisa Foster, the third and youngest member of our party, shows up full of enthusiasm. "What route are we taking?" she wants to know. Jim tells her "The Notch Couloir."

Unfamiliar with that route, I suggest we do the North Face, a climb involving a couple of roped pitches but not too difficult. I used that route on my first trip up the mountain years ago. Jim agrees, figuring it will increase our chance of reaching the summit.

We strap snowshoes to our packs. The trail climbs rapidly, angling through a spire forest of Englemann spruce and subalpine fir. Yesterday's snow has added another layer to the snowpack. The 14,256-foot summit lies seven and a half miles away by trail and nearly 5,000 feet above us.

Crossing a creek completely buried under snow, we listen to the muffled flow of water below. Jim points out the tracks of a snowshoe hare as we pass a line of yeti-size tracks left by the snow surveyors I'd accompanied earlier.

Snow surveyors take snowpack readings from hundreds of sites throughout the western mountains. "It's not just the depth of the snow that's important for stream flow predictions," Paul Gallegos told me, "but the density, the moisture content. Many people depend on the runoff from the winter snowpack. Everyone wants to know what will come down and when it will come down."

Paul and his partner, Don Graffis, conduct their snow surveys for the Natural Resources Conservation Service. The three of us hiked up the trail close to timberline, stopping at a yellow snow-course marker. Putting on their long, upturned snowshoes, the two surveyors left the trail to take samples along the course.

"Farmers are waiting for our report," Paul said. "They base what to plant on it and how much to plant. We can give indications, but it's not really predictable. There are too many variables. It depends on not only what's up there but when it comes down. You can't get excited by what's there now because it can change tomorrow."

Jim, Lisa, and I pass the surveyors' course and continue the steady grind up the mountain. A sky, solid blue, hangs above the tips of the evergreens. Birds sing and flit among the branches as clumps of snow unload in puffs of white dust. In weather like this it's hard to believe that 48 people have lost their lives on Longs Peak.

Switchbacking higher, we pause to strap on the snow-shoes. Yesterday's forecast had called for another storm front

Steam engulfs bathers and readers in the hot springs at Glenwood Springs (right). Skiers and hikers often end their day in the mountains by soaking in the mineral springs or by relaxing in the vapor cave at Ouray (below).

to move in today, so the mild weather is unexpected. "We're lucky," Jim says, smiling. "You don't know how lucky. This is just a real gift."

Moving higher, I glance up and Longs Peak is suddenly there, a classic peak standing boldly above the skyline. "That's the finest mountain on the planet," Detterline says.

New snow dusts the ancient rock of the crag, a solid mass of granite 1.45 billion years old. Explorer John Wesley Powell made the first recorded ascent of Longs Peak in 1868, and Enos Mills the first winter climb 35 years later. But Arapaho Indians may have reached the top before either of them. According to oral tradition, they once climbed the peak to trap eagles. We might have a chance to try for the summit ourselves. "It's looking good," Jim says.

The Diamond, a sheer wall dominating the 2,000-foot East Face, is one of the highest cliffs in the Rockies, a training ground for expeditions from around the world. Jim has scaled it many times and has climbed Longs Peak 80 times, in all the months of the year.

Recent storms have loaded the East Face ledges and ravines with snow, but the steepest rock hangs bare, stark gray. I stand at tree line studying the Notch Couloir, the route we almost took. It's an impressive chute of snow and ice to the left of the Diamond, a white scar cutting vertically down the face. As I watch, a snowslide pours down the couloir and spills over a cliff in a cascade of powder.

"A spindrift avalanche," Jim says. The fresh snow has unloaded, threatening deeper slab avalanches. We'd come close to being on that route at the wrong time. He glances at me with a smile, remembering the change of plans. "That was a good call."

An avalanche once caught Detterline during a search for a missing climber. He was nearing the top of Longs when a news helicopter, hovering nearby, triggered a slide. "I was completely engulfed in snow," he remembers. "It went everywhere—eyes, nose, mouth. I was beginning to suffocate. A hundred feet down the chute I managed to roll over and slam in my ice ax. The slide tore past and ran another 1,500 feet before it stopped."

Wind and extreme cold have beveled the edge of the forest where we stand, forming a transition zone called krummholz, German for crooked wood. Full trees taper off to stunted outliers. A line of half-trees, rooted on the cutting edge, grows branches only on the leeward side. Other trees hug the ground, clustering for protection.

Above the krummholz lies the alpine tundra, beginning about 11,000 feet. It's a treeless expanse of sedges and grasses, moss cushions, and lichens. Much of it now lies under the snowpack, protected from the most extreme weather. Skirting Mills Moraine, we cross a snowfield. Jim stops suddenly. "Do you see it?" he asks. "A ptarmigan."

"Where?"

"Straight ahead. And another. And another higher up." I spot a bird sitting as white and rounded as a snowball. Another pecks at its foot feathers, cleaning away the snow. In winter their toenails work as snowshoes by growing comb-like teeth. White-tailed ptarmigans are among the few birds to live above tree line year-round. They appear soft and defenseless, yet manage to survive sub-zero weather and hurricane-force winds.

A blizzard overtakes a steam locomotive as it winds along the Animas River on the tracks of the Durango & Silverton Narrow Gauge Railroad. Rails only three feet apart, and lightweight rolling stock—easier and cheaper to build and maintain than standard-gauge lines—linked many mountain towns during mining's turn-of-the-century heyday.

They have come to terms with winter, using its whiteness for camouflage and its snow for insulation. We pass another ptarmigan digging a snow cave, preparing for an impending change in the weather that we haven't noticed.

A single cloud begins to coalesce in the gulf of air below the summit. Only one cloud appears, but it may be a forerunner of more to come. We snowshoe up a bowl of pure, untracked snow on a spur ridge of Mount Lady Washington. Taking a steep line up the slope, Jim pauses briefly with each step, using the mountaineer's rest step. All around us lie mountains with rough contours blunted by the snow.

High clouds slide in above, and the wind picks up. Clouds begin to surge over Longs Peak, obscuring the summit. A storm must be approaching from the west, screened from view by the mountains. We stop below the ridge crest to put on another layer of clothing. "It's going to be brutal," Jim warns.

He pulls on a pile balaclava and a park service hat with long earflaps. Lisa, wearing a mountain parka and shell pants, fits snow goggles over a wool cap. The air temperature takes a dive. A rivulet of sweat has run down the lens of my sunglasses and frozen solid. Exposed fingers turn numb.

Winds hit even before we top the ridge. "Typical Longs Peak weather," Jim says as a gust snatches the rest of his words. We reach the Boulder Field where slabs of jagged rock poke above an expanse of snow. As we cross the snowfield in a running ground blizzard, a powerful gust momentarily stops us in our tracks. We hunch over with our backs to the blast, waiting until it passes. Our tracks blow away behind us. Snow spirals upward. The storm has arrived in full force. Snow sweeps the ground; clouds fly through the sky; everything is moving but the mountains themselves. We finally halt, still 1,500 feet below the summit.

Studying the route, Jim estimates we need four hours to reach the top—if the weather doesn't get worse. It's already past noon. That means a night descent, rappelling in the dark under blizzard conditions. Jim delays a decision, hoping the storm will lessen. Longs Peak is one of the world's windiest places with 220-miles-per-hour gusts recorded on the summit. Due to the extreme conditions only 5 to 10 percent of the winter attempts succeed in reaching the top.

As we wait, Detterline tells about a rescue he once led. It began when winds blew a climber off the West Face of Longs. He fell 70 feet, landing on a ledge and suffering a depressed skull fracture. A chopper took Jim to the summit. It was too windy to land, so he jumped from a hover. He rounded up volunteers already on the peak since it was too dangerous to bring in his full team. Unable to evacuate the victim by air, they had to carry him off the mountain in a litter, slammed by hundred-miles-per-hour gusts. "It was a grueling night."

After 12 hours the rescue party had only descended as far as a shelter above the Boulder Field. The wind had blown one rescuer off his feet, and a falling rock had struck another. Everyone was exhausted. Jim called the volunteers together and told them they were released from their duty. "Anybody who wants to leave," he said, "can leave now."

One of the rescuers asked if there was still a chance to save the injured climber. "I told them he has a better chance if we keep him moving," Jim says. "They all walked out of the shelter, ready to go. It was the most incredible thing I've seen in the mountains." The climber survived.

Visibility continues to deteriorate as clouds stream across the rock face. Under these conditions, our only real choice is to descend. "I hate turning back after so much effort to reach this point," Jim says, pausing to look up at the summit. "Let's get into our packs."

Pelted by blowing ice and sand-charged blasts, we file off the mountain. Clouds slide down the high ridges, closing the door behind us. Snow begins to fall as we descend, turning heavy before we reach the trailhead. We have spent a full day in the mountains, moving steadily from dawn to dusk, but we're not done yet.

"Leave your gear on," Jim tells us when we reach the cabin. "We're heading to Ed's Cantina."

FOLLOWING PAGES: Wrenched upward in an expanse of sharp-cut peaks, the San Juan Mountains cover 10,000 square miles, to form the most extensive range in the American Rockies.

Basque sheepherder Julio Rivera (below) greets his four-footed friends at a camp outside the town of Telluride in the San Juans. As fall arrives, a river of sheep (opposite) pours down a mountain road, leaving the high-country pastures behind.

FOLLOWING PAGES: Quaking aspens, with their trunks chalk-white or yellow-green, reach toward an autumn sky.

The still waters of an alpine pool reflect a rugged skyline high in the Rockies (below). Morning sunlight, streaming through the branches of an Englemann spruce, (opposite) breaks over a ridge in the San Juan Mountains.

FOLLOWING PAGES: *Warm golden light bathes a horse grazing in a wheat field.*

73

Yellow blossoms of shrubby cinquefoil (opposite) burst from among the rocks in an alpine basin of Rocky Mountain National Park. More than a third of the park lies above tree line, where tundra predominates. A handful of Colorado blue columbine (right) finds shelter from the harsh high-country weather. Southwest of Aspen, early snow covers the banded face of the Maroon Bells (above). Winter moves down the mountain as fall colors endure on the valley floor.

*Gateway to the
Rockies, Denver
International Airport
glows from within at
dusk (left). The roof
angles upward in
multiple peaks, echo-
ing the craggy skyline
to the west. While
many visitors enter
the Rockies on foot
and skis, some float
in—like a paraglider
soaring over the slopes
of Aspen Mountain.*

Strong and surefooted, Belgian horses pull a feed sleigh through heavy snow near Steamboat Springs. Despite the stormy northern Colorado weather, ranchers Raymond Gray and John Daughenbaugh deliver hay to their hungry cattle. On another ranch, mountain snows bury an old barn.

*Evening light strikes
Lizard Head (top),
south of Telluride.
As the day ends, the
lights of the old
mining town sparkle
within the steep-walled
valley (left). A century
ago, after his first
bank robbery, Butch
Cassidy galloped out
of Telluride with a
posse on his heels.
Skiers (opposite) find
a quieter way to see
the high country on
the deep snow of Red
Mountain Pass.*

*FOLLOWING PAGES:
Heavy snowfall veils
a tepee pitched in the
North Star Preserve
outside Aspen.*

Mountain Frontier

*Immense boulders appear to defy gravity at
Vedauwoo in the Laramie Mountains. This eastern range of the Rockies
rises from the high plains of eastern Wyoming.*

*So like its old self does the sage-brush
seem when revisited, that you wait
for the horseman to appear.*

Owen Wister

HE FORCES WERE just awesome," says geologist David Love. He crumples the placemat in front of him to demonstrate the compression of deeply buried rock. He is describing tectonic events that occurred during the creation of the Rocky Mountains.

On my way north, I've stopped to talk with this noted field geologist at his home in Laramie, Wyoming. Mountains bracket the town, with the Medicine Bows rising to the west and the Laramie Mountains stretching to the east. These last traces of the Front Range dovetail with the high plains of Wyoming.

"In the break between the southern and northern Rockies," David says, "you have a jumble. We live in a geologically complicated area, the result of two gigantic forces going in different directions."

Cowboy-hatted visitors to Yellowstone National Park watch Old Faithful shoot a column of steam and superheated water into the blue sky. The world's first national park, Yellowstone lies in Wyoming, Idaho, and Montana— Old Faithful is in Wyoming. In the park, six geysers regularly erupt a hundred feet or higher.

Raised on a cattle ranch, David earned a doctorate at Yale. He returned to crisscross the state on foot, horseback, and truck during his geologic mapping of Wyoming.

"The settlement of the West," says David, "was determined largely by two things: the water and the geology. There are a lot of sedimentary rocks that don't grow grass; they provide no nutrients at all. But all along the Sweetwater River the soil was good, the water was good. So the Oregon Trail went around the Front Range and up the Sweetwater River, along the top of a partly buried mountain range that long ago had sagged 3,000 feet. South Pass is a swale; there were no mountains to cross. This was the first practical way to the West."

Early overland travel funneled through the breach between the Southern Rockies and the ranges farther north. Traders and Mormon refugees, gold seekers and Pony Express riders joined a flood of emigrants pouring through South Pass.

In the peak years of 1850 and 1851, "50,000 people and 150,000 critters per year," David says, "were concentrated in a 30-mile-wide strip along the Oregon Trail. The result was total devastation of the rangeland. But it's come back."

After saying goodbye, I walk to the door past a painting of a mountain weathered to its core. Earlier I had glanced at the same canvas and seen a landscape, solid and unmoving. Now, after talking geology, I saw the scene pitch and toss as rock masses thrust upward in great crustal movements. Expand the time frame, and mountains begin to move.

Deep deposits once buried all but the highest peaks of the ancient Rockies, encasing them in layered sediments turned to stone. As the land lifted, about 10 million years ago, the stream gradients steepened and the rivers gained force. They stripped back the overlying deposits, uncovering the ancestral mountains buried for 20 million years or more.

*L*EAVING LARAMIE, I follow the old highway that loops northwest through the grasslands. Connecting roads will carry me to the Wind River country through a region that takes its identity not only from the lay of the land but from the people living close to it.

Snow has melted from the plains, releasing the grass, long buried. A few flowers have opened, perhaps too soon as the season totters. In the distance, a snow squall crosses the Medicine Bows, smudging the dark profile of Elk Mountain at the tip of the range. It's springtime in the Rockies.

Miles stretch away in every direction as grasslands roll down to the town of Medicine Bow with a population of less than 400. Pickups and dusty sedans wait in front of the Virginian Hotel, parked nose-in at the board sidewalk like horses crowding a watering trough. Across the street, a monument of petrified wood commemorates the town's literary legacy. Medicine Bow was the setting for Owen Wister's 1902 novel, *The Virginian,* a story that helped to transform the cowboy into an American legend. It was inside a Medicine Bow saloon that the book's hero responded to an insult with the classic line, "When you call me that, *smile!*"

Wister's best-selling novel popularized the American West at the moment it seemed to be gone forever. "It is a vanished world," he wrote in a note to readers. "No journeys, save those which memory can take, will bring you to it now. . . . So like its old self does the sage-brush seem when revisited, that you wait for the horseman to appear. But he will never come again. He rides in his historic yesterday."

Flakes of snow scatter from the gray sky over South Pass, melting on the pavement as they land. The bulk of the Wind River Range lies to the north. Sagebrush plains roll up one side of the Continental Divide, only 7,412 feet high at this point, and down the other. South Pass was the primary route across the Rocky Mountains for horse-drawn wagons. Here west-moving settlers crossed a threshold, entering a new land where the rivers flowed toward the Pacific.

The highway descends into the Green River country where fur trappers, traders, and Indians gathered for the last mountain man rendezvous in 1840. I drive through Pinedale, a small trading center for ranches and a jumping-off point for those heading into the high country. "All the Civilization You Need," the welcome sign reads. A few miles west, I turn toward the log post office at Cora. The land beyond reaches to the wild Wind Rivers.

A run of sawtooth mountains spreads from the southeast to the northwest. Still buried under snow, almost two dozen peaks climb above 13,000 feet with Gannett Peak, the highest in Wyoming, topping out at 13,804 feet.

The Flying U Ranch lies near Cora on the New Fork, a branch of the Green River. I stop at a log bunkhouse built in the 19th century. Next to it, my old friend George Renner is splitting stovewood with a double-bit ax. He has wintered here on the Noble family ranch in a canvas-covered wagon.

A cedar-chest maker, George, grips the ax handle with strong, gnarled hands. His full beard tumbles over a red bandana wrapped around his neck. His hair dangles waist-length, tied back with an elk thong. Now in his mid-70s, Rawhide George grew up on a ranch below the Bighorn Mountains. His first job, he tells me, paid ten cents a day.

Next to the wagon, a canvas awning shades a workbench built for mobility. Mounted on the side of an old truck,

Peaks of the Teton Range thrust above the Snake River in Wyoming. At their foot, 93-year-old Mardy Murie (opposite) sits on the porch of her log home. The celebrated conservationist continues to deliver a simple message: "Beauty itself is a resource; it must be preserved."

it can be folded up when on the road. Spokeshaves and hand planes fill the shelves; each tool has its place. The craftsman carves wooden hinges for his chests, selecting each piece of wood for its strength and beauty. It's exacting work that he insists on doing the right way.

We enter the warmth of the wagon. Wooden bows arc overhead, supporting the canvas top. George has designed the interior for close-quarters living. No space is wasted. He pulls out two folding stools and sets them next to a scaled-down table. A compact cookstove is tucked near the door. All the furnishings have been handcrafted with a simplicity matching the spare beauty of the natural surroundings. Sitting in the wagon, his home on wheels for 30 years, George tells a story.

"When I was young, I kept looking for someone who could teach me something," he begins. "On our ranch we had all kinds of men to do the cowboying—sailors, lumbermen, world travelers. I talked to them all. Many of them had been all over the world, but they hadn't learned anything from it. Everyone except for Charlie Paterson who was half Sioux. I learned a lot from Charlie—how to hunt elk and a philosophy of how to take care of yourself."

At some point in the conversation, the talk comes around to animals. It often does in this country. Recently, wildlife managers released gray wolves in Yellowstone National Park, returning them to the wild. Emotions are running high on both sides of the issue. Already ranchers have shot one of the animals who strayed outside the park boundaries.

But George is puzzled by the controversy. He says gray wolves have been passing through these mountains for a long time. Years ago he set up his outfit in the Targhee country west

of the Tetons, an area heavily grazed by sheep. When a sudden
July storm dropped more than two feet of snow, he headed out
for a look, taking along his rifle. In the mountains above camp,
he crossed paths with a wolf who had recently had pups.

"We saw each other at the same instant," he remembers.
"Oh, she was gorgeous in all that fresh snow. She was looking
right at me. 'You ol' sweetheart,' I told her. 'Now don't you be
afraid there, you pretty thing. I won't touch a hair on your
head. Go on now and be on your way.' "

Under the glow of the lantern, George takes down his
fiddle and plays an old tune. His foot taps to the swing of the
bow as the notes of "Soldier's Joy" fill the wagon. Soon he
pulls out the lower bunk, set on trundles, and turns in. I climb
into the top bunk under heavy blankets.

Next morning the wind carries the smell of singed fur,
thick and acrid. It's branding time on a blustery spring day
with snow clouds circling the horizon. Climbing a pole fence, I
enter a corral filled with men, women, and children working
the calves. It's a gathering of the Noble clan. Some of the men
wear leather chaps and cowboy hats, and some, with an eye
toward the weather, have on winter caps. I shake hands with
rancher Dick Noble and join the flankers.

Calves bunch together on the far side of the corral,
bawling for their mothers who wait in the next pen and add
their moaning calls to the tumult. A cowboy on horseback
swings the catch-rope over his head and lassos one of the
calves. He drags it closer to the branding irons. The black calf
bucks and lurches, pulling against the rope. "We got a wild
one," the rider shouts.

On foot, a man flanks the heifer calf, flipping it to the

ground. His partner pins the head while he stretches out a hind leg and braces his foot against the other leg. Tina, the rancher's daughter, administers a vaccination shot and her sister-in-law tags the ear. If it's a bull calf, the women will castrate it. Dick walks over with a red-hot iron. A former bishop of the local Mormon church, he is the third of five generations of Nobles who have lived on this land. His grandfather came West on a cattle drive, got involved in a shoot-out over a gold mine, and ended up homesteading on the New Fork. A trace of smoke curls up as he sets his brand into the animal's hide.

Andy Nelson sits with legs spraddled and his four-year-old son in his lap. Both hang onto the leg of a burly calf. Next to them, I grip the hind foot of another animal as Mardy Nelson and her friend Bonnie, both nine-year olds, struggle to hold down the head. They've been roping and flanking the smaller calves all morning, enjoying the commotion. Dick presses down with the branding iron. The girls turn their heads away from the smoke as he sings a line from "Smoke Gets in Your Eyes."

Around noon a curtain of snow sweeps across the distant expanse, and another squall blows straight toward the corrals. Pellets of dry snow rattle against the roof of a pickup and sprinkle the hats and shoulders of the horsemen. No one pays much attention. The work proceeds at a steady pace. Inside the ranch house, Dick's wife, Louise, has been busy all morning fixing a spread to feed the crew after the work is done.

When the branding ends, one of the hands opens a gate to reunite the calves with their mothers. All the helpers mount up to drive the cattle to pasture. The herd trails past a beaver-slide stacker, a wooden ramp used for piling loose hay. Snowy peaks stack up behind it. A horseman gives a whoop, and another joins in as Dick hollers, "Give 'em hell, cowboys!"

*T*RAVELING THROUGH the Wind River country, I found people who draw strength from traditions. One couple, Snook and Evalyn Moore, live much like the pioneers who homesteaded these parts. Wyoming has always been Snook's home, but Evalyn found her way here by chance.

During the Depression, she knew she would have to leave California to find a teaching job. She took out a map. And closed her eyes. After randomly jabbing it with a pen, she wrote to each town hit by a drop of ink. Evalyn ended up in a one-room schoolhouse on the upper Green River. At a Christmas dance, the school teacher from California met the Wyoming broncobuster Snook Moore and fell in love.

Sixty years later they are still together and, as I learned, snowed in at their cabin in the Wind Rivers. I've arranged to visit them through their friend Sava Malachowski, a documentary filmmaker and former activist with the Polish Solidarity Union. "Snook is the last of the legends," Sava tells me.

We follow the road along the Green River, not yet charged by spring runoff. The water loops quietly through the soft purples and oranges of the willow thickets. Snow has melted from south-facing banks but lies heaped on gravel bars in the river. Where a deep drift blocks the way, Sava parks the truck to wait for a snowmobile to shuttle us 12 miles to the Moore Ranch. On the edge of the road stands a grove of bare white aspens, rising from a mound of glacial till. A boulder, left behind by retreating ice and worn smooth and round, lies at the center of the trees. Overhead, a pair of sandhill cranes fly with their long necks stretched skyward and their slender legs trailing behind. They call and call again, breaking the stillness of a winter grown old.

Soon the snowmobile arrives, driven by Daniel McNeilly, a young ranch hand from North Carolina. I straddle the machine behind the driver; Sava will take the second run. We fly along the flats at full throttle, slowing as the track winds into the hills. Daniel drops me off at the ranch and turns back. Half a dozen log cabins set among the aspens huddle together. Horse-drawn implements for cutting, raking, and stacking hay fill a nearby shed. The Gros Ventre Mountains, obscured by a rise of land, lie to the northwest. Across the valley stands the western wall of the Wind Rivers, the ridgeline vague in the blank white of snowfields set against snowclouds.

Two dogs lying on the porch wag their tails as I cross a footbridge to the main cabin. Smoke rises from the stovepipe. Entering through the kitchen, I find Evalyn, 92 years old, doing the laundry on a woodstove. Wearing a checkered apron, she scrubs the clothes on a washboard. This woman, who loves flowers and classical music, looks up with a warm smile. "I don't want to shake hands," she says, "give me a hug."

Using a cane, she leads me into the next room where Snook is peeling potatoes. The old guide sits hunched over his work, wearing a flannel shirt and a rodeo trophy buckle on his belt. Snook looks up slowly, his eyes a pale blue, cloudless.

Old injuries, coupled with arthritis, have slowed him down. Nearly 80 years old, he estimates he's fractured almost every bone in his body at least once, mostly when he was breaking horses. "Yep, them was the good ol' days," he says with a twinkle in his eye.

For many years he guided hunters into the mountains. "Those Winds are something," he says. "I hunted in those mountains for 49 falls, and I learned how rough they was."

FOLLOWING PAGES: Fumaroles steam and geysers spew in Yellowstone's Upper Geyser Basin. This thermal landscape along the Firehole River contains the world's highest concentration of geysers.

During elk season, Snook would lead his clients to a base camp, hunt with them all day, and go back at night to pack in the meat. "Did you ever get lost?" I ask him.

"I don't think he could get lost," Evalyn says, "and we've gone to some wild places." Snook smiles at Evalyn, remembering the time she tried her hardest to get him lost just to see if it could be done.

"Well," he says in a slow, easy cadence, "I guess I never did get lost. But I should have."

The three of us sit in handmade chairs, the backs and seats laced with rawhide in a snowshoe pattern—a pattern the Moores know well. For nearly 20 years, often on snowshoes, they fed elk during the winter for the state.

Evalyn always wanted to raise a bear cub or fawn, but Snook wouldn't let her. "He told me it's not right," she says. "You do that and they don't belong to the wild any more, and they don't belong to the tame."

But one day a game warden stopped at their place with an orphaned elk calf. Snook reluctantly agreed to let Evalyn try to care for it. She bottle-fed the elk they named Butch, and soon he was following them everywhere. When Snook took the pack train out, the elk would trail right behind the horses. Each time they drove to town, Butch trotted after their truck for miles and always stopped to wait for their return.

The next year, Snook knew it was past time for the pet elk to go back to the wild. He tried to lure him to the feeding grounds, but Butch sensed he was up to something and refused to follow. Finally Snook loaded the animal on the hay sled and dropped him off with the others. Next fall, the couple glanced up to see Butch heading toward the house, leading a herd of 15 elk. Snook walked over to him and scratched his antlers. They didn't see him again until the following winter.

One day, on the way to town, the Moores spotted an animal lying on the river ice. It was Butch. The elk had been shot. He was alive but couldn't stand. "He wanted us to help him," Evalyn says, the memory still painful. "He held his antlers back so they wouldn't hurt us. The two of us lifted him up, but he fell back. A bullet had lodged in his backbone. It had paralyzed his hind end. Snook stayed with him, bringing him water and hay for three or four days until he died."

"I wish I tried taking that bullet out," Snook says with deep regret. "Maybe I could have saved him."

Wet snowflakes begin to fall as we say goodbye. "Come back in the fall," Evalyn says. "It's a golden world, it truly is."

Farther west, the Snake River sweeps around a bend and turns again, curving toward the sudden uplift of the Tetons. Above the river, immense planes of sheared rock heave upward into crags whitened by snow. Grand Teton, the focal peak, thrusts more than a mile above the floor of Jackson Hole, reaching a height of 13,770 feet.

Landscape photographer Ansel Adams set up his tripod at this viewpoint half a century ago and captured a timeless image of the Tetons. In the 1970s, aided by the National Geographic Society, scientists chose photographs of our home planet to accompany the Voyager mission. The spacecraft has now left the solar system, heading toward deep space. Adams' photo of the Tetons was one of the images stowed on board as a message for any extraterrestrial life Voyager might encounter.

WALKING ALONG the Gros Ventre River, not far from where it joins the Snake, I talk with my friend Jeremy Schmidt. Jeremy began living in this country as a park ranger and now writes about the Rockies. Trees string down the open slopes of Blacktail Butte, behind us, with tracers of snow lining the gullies. The contours are soft and flowing in contrast to the Teton crest breaking above it. We pause to look back at the skyline, glacier-carved into dramatic peaks. This is the youngest range in the Rockies, formed nine million years ago.

"No matter how many times I see them," Jeremy says, "they never get any less unreal."

Detouring around a cow moose scrutinizing us from the sagebrush, we intersect a major elk trail. Tracks pointing north ford the river where meltwater riffles over cobblestones. Leading away from the National Elk Refuge, the trail climbs the bank, churned to mud by the animals' passage, and enters Grand Teton National Park. A herd of 16,000 elk, one of the world's largest, winters in and around Jackson Hole, many of them on the protected feeding ground between the town of Jackson and the park. With snow lingering in the high country, they have been slow in dispersing to their summer ranges.

"I like the spring migration better than the fall," Jeremy says. "Things are greening up, the cow elk are pregnant. In the fall the elk are fighting a guerrilla war. They wait for night to make a run for the refuge. They know that when they cross the line, they're safe. I like spring the best."

With their migration routes restricted and much of their traditional winter range now developed, many of the elk would starve unless fed throughout the winter. "The park has this lofty ideal of natural regulation," Jeremy says, "but there is nothing natural about how the ecosystem is managed."

He gives an example. "In Yellowstone they have worked for more than fifty years to bring back the cutthroat trout. The significance of the cutthroat lies in how other animals in the ecosystem—grizzlies, otters, and pelicans—rely on them. The park has done a magnificent job in bringing them back."

But recently someone planted lake trout in Yellowstone Lake without the Park Service's knowledge. The exotic fish now threaten the native cutthroat, so gill netting is under way to thin the lake trout population. "Some of these ecological programs are amazingly fragile, easily subverted," Jeremy says.

We leave the river and drive past an abandoned farm on Antelope Flats. The roof peak of the barn angles as sharply as the mountain summits behind it. In front of us straggles a line of bison, plodding across the road to rejoin the main herd of about 100 animals. With their winter coats beginning to molt, they have a tattered look. The largest free-ranging herds travel through the Yellowstone country north of the Tetons.

Last winter I followed geologist Rick Hutchinson along the Firehole River in Yellowstone National Park, his home for 25 years. He stepped off the ski track where the trail began the climb to Grants Pass. The bark of a lodgepole pine next to him had been rubbed off, leaving a hair caught in a splinter.

"Bison," said Rick. Hydrothermal heat keeps the river from freezing, allowing a handful of bulls to winter in the thermal basin on the headwaters of the Firehole. In 1902, the year *The Virginian* was published, fewer than 50 bison remained in the park; today they number about 4,000.

Starting at Old Faithful, I was accompanying the park geologist on a research trip into the backcountry. He conducts his fieldwork throughout the year, usually traveling alone into remote areas. We were skiing to the Shoshone thermal basin where Rick planned to study geyser eruptions.

Rick unrolled his climbing skins, long strips designed to stick onto ski bottoms. The nap of the fabric allows a skier to glide forward but grips the snow in the opposite direction to prevent a backward slide. After securing the tails with duct tape, he stepped into the bindings and began the ascent.

To keep the weight off his shoulders, Rick pulled his pack behind him on a sled. He wore a salt-and-pepper beard and a trapper-style winter hat with the sides turned up.

"That ridge ahead," he said, indicating the crest of the pass, "is the Continental Divide." Snow buried the summit. Eight feet of accumulation is common at Yellowstone, with drifts almost twice as deep, but so far the snowpack had reached a depth of only six feet.

The trail wrapped down the far side of the pass in long switchbacks, dodging trees with drooping, snow-weighted limbs. When the track reached the head of Shoshone Creek, it leveled out across a snowfield. An elemental white covered all surfaces, with pillows of snow curling over the creek banks.

For several miles we descended along a steep canyon wall. To keep from sliding into the creek below, we planted our ski edges deeply into the crusted slope. After a long push, we broke into the open. Before us emerged a hill of green—it was moss growing on slopes kept snow-free by the heat of the ground. We had been enclosed in white all day, so the green appeared intensely alive. "It looks like Ireland," Rick said.

Before we reached the thermal springs, the air became heavy and sulfurous. Ahead, steam plumes drifted eerily from dozens of vents. Removing our skis and packs, we crossed the basin, one of more than 120 thermal areas in the park.

Ground heat had melted the snowbanks, carving their edges into curves and scallops. The closest trees stood encased by rime ice where steam had frozen. Buffalo scat lay about on the open ground by the vents. Near a flock of Canada geese, a solitary bison pivoted his massive head toward us, only mildly curious, then turned back to the grass in front of him.

Some of the geyser vents had formed a mineral coating of finely-beaded sinter in the splash zone around their bases. A few mud pots tossed bubbling splats of gray mud. A single strand of bubbles rose from the bottom of a clear blue pool; others roiled and spattered. Each pool had its own tint, ranging from reds and yellows to tea black. "Most of the colors are biological," Rick said, "bacteria and algae."

Steam billowed up from an erupting geyser named Little Giant. Other vents sputtered and hissed. "Each spring," Rick

Clouds of steam drift from a breach in the frozen surface of Jackson Lake. Lying below the Tetons, the lake formed behind a moraine left by a melting valley glacier.

said, "has its own sound. Close your eyes and listen."

Gurgles and gulps and blurbles drifted in from different directions in a soothing mix. We paused at a blue pool, deep and hot, about 182 degrees. Then we reached Minute Man, the geyser Rick had come to study. The thermal feature was named for its frequent eruptions, occurring at intervals of about one to three minutes.

As we watched, the vent erupted with a roar. A column of scalding water spouted into the cold air with a steamy cloud climbing even higher. Deep below the surface, water becomes heated above the surface boiling point by partially molten rock. A geyser forms when this superheated water nears the surface and pressure is suddenly released. The expanding jet of steam pushes water before it as it shoots through a surface vent.

The geologist stood still and attentive before the geyser as clouds of steam swirled around him. He noted the interval between bursts, their duration, and the extent of the splashing droplets. He needed to predict the right moment to place a thermistor, attached to an instrument he had programmed to record the temperature every ten seconds.

As another eruption subsided, Rick dashed in and set the thermistor on the rim of the vent. He had only moments to weight it down with rocks. Timing things just right, he placed the last stone and stepped back as the geyser blew again.

*B*Y EARLY EVENING we had returned to our packs and skied to the edge of the lake ice. The surface of Shoshone, the largest backcountry lake in the park, lay table flat and untracked. Several feet of crusted snow had accumulated on top. Rick led along a set route, avoiding the hazards where the heat of submerged springs had thinned the ice. Tendrils of steam rose through holes in the surface. A flock of trumpeter swans floated in an open lead nearby. One of them called out, sounding two brassy notes as it watched our passage.

To the south rolled the shoulder of the Pitchstone Plateau. Yellowstone is a land of high plateaus, generally without the dramatic relief found in the Teton and Wind River Ranges. We continued on a straight course, skiing for several miles across the white expanse. Ahead, Rick let his skis ease to a standstill. "It's peaceful," he said as I pulled next to him. We listened for a moment to the absence of sound.

In the distance, a forested headland reached far into the lake, forming a narrows. The ranger-patrol cabin lay somewhere on this side of it, but it was difficult to pick out in the flat light. Just as daylight faded, Rick found the shelter behind a screen of trees and buried under snow. After shoveling clear the doorway, we stomped our boots and entered the cabin. Rick started a fire in the woodstove, and I shook out my sleeping bag in the loft above.

By morning a blanket of thermal fog had settled over the lake basin. The snow-covered surface merged with the sky in an unbroken field of white. When the fog burned off, we clamped into our skis and glided across the lake through the bright whiteness of an unusually mild winter day.

As we entered the geyser basin, sunlight filtered through the steam clouds, glinting and breaking into rainbow bands. Ephydrid flies flittered above the outflow channels, staying close to the microbial mats for food and warmth. Nearby a few green plants—a ground-hugging stonecrop and the leaves of a yellow monkeyflower—had pierced the surface.

After Rick checked his instrument at Minute Man, the two of us wandered onto a ridge of glacial debris, thermally cemented. Steam rose from acid pools as a fumarole hissed, shooting sideways like a puncture in the sidewall of a tire. Sulfur ringed the throat of the vent with bright yellow crystals. Walking over this heated ground gave me a visceral sense of crossing a very thin crust of the earth's surface.

At the cabin that evening, Rick talked about the summer of 1988, when dozens of wildfires swept through the forests of Yellowstone. They joined into major blazes that eventually burned more than a third of the park.

The fire jumped most of Old Faithful Village, sparing the historic inn but destroying cabins and other structures. That night, Rick walked down through the geyser basin. "It was magical," he said. "The whoosh of trees torching, the crash of falling lodgepoles, the gurgle and hiss of the geysers. Snags would flare up on the surrounding ridges, and the Firehole River glowed orange-red, reflecting the fires. It was amazing to see the power of nature."

Retrieving the instrument the next day, we retraced our outward trail and headed back to Old Faithful. By early afternoon we were passing through a skeleton forest of burned-over lodgepole pines. The gray trunks stood straight and bare against a gray sky. We crested the ridge above the village and pointed our skis down the Howard Eaton Trail. Rick disappeared ahead, descending through a run of corkscrew turns. I caught up at a point where the tree cover thinned.

Sunlight broke through, streaming into the valley of the Firehole River below us. We could see the rooftops of the village and the location of Old Faithful beyond. As we watched, the famous geyser suddenly erupted, sending a pure white plume of steam far into the winter sky.

FOLLOWING PAGES: Rock climbers rest under weathered boulders of granite that formed 1.4 billion years ago. The Vedauwoo rocks near Laramie take their name from an Arapaho Indian word for "earthborn."

Eroded hills (below)
break through clouds
covering Wyoming's
Great Divide Basin,
a land where wild
horses roam. Backed
by helicopters, wran-
glers herd mustangs
into a box canyon
(opposite). With the
chase over, horses
huddle together before
being transported for
later adoption.

Clouds thin to reveal a mustang like a silvery apparition. Wranglers from the Bureau of

Land Management regularly capture wild horses to prevent their overgrazing and starving.

Snowmelt cascades
into alpine lakes, lur-
ing fly fishermen to
the high Wind River
Range in Wyoming.
Legendary guide
Snook Moore once
hooked a rainbow
trout in a remote
Wind River lake.
"What he weighed I
had no idea," he said.
"But, by golly, he just
about peeled my reel
that first run!"

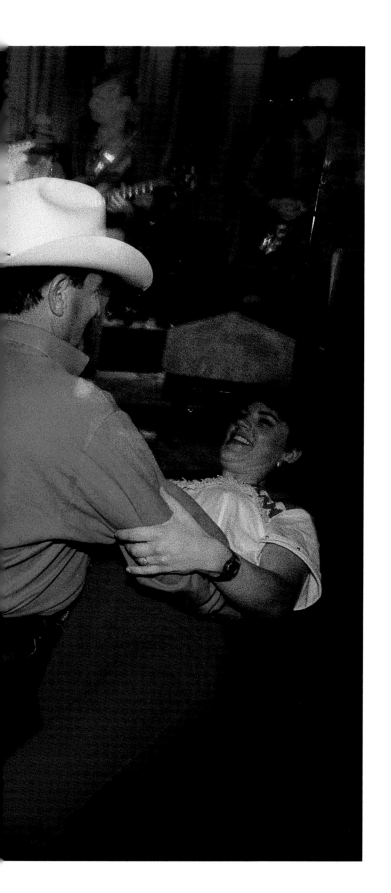

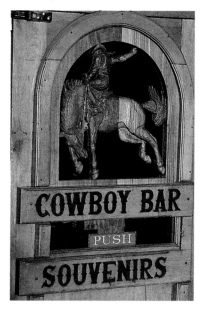

Time off for folks at Jackson Hole. Western dancers two-step the night away, while beyond the door of the Cowboy Bar, a horseman can feel right at home by mounting a saddle-rigged barstool. At the nearby town of Moose, a contemplative cowboy stands as an icon of the West—both old and new.

Those who winter in the Rockies find their own remedies for cabin fever. After climbing a ridge above Jackson Hole, a skier (opposite) descends the nearly vertical wall of a couloir. At the base of the mountain, hats fly as riders pull skiers in the Hell-Bent-for-Leather Race.

FOLLOWING PAGES: In the early morning, winter light washes across a snow-buried spur of the Teton Range. Here the winds have formed a sharp cornice along the sinuous ridgeline.

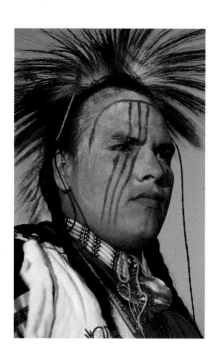

Spinning gracefully, a young Indian girl dances within a swirl of fringe. In the Mountain West, Native Americans often gather at pow-wows to dance and visit old friends. Face colorfully painted, a traditional dancer watches other per-formers at a powwow in Cody, Wyoming.

Grand Prismatic
Spring attracted artists
more than a century
ago. Thomas Moran,
with the expedition of
geologist-explorer
Ferdinand Hayden,
sketched the hot
spring's bright rings in
1871. During winter,
thermal basins draw

bison (opposite) to the
warm microclimates.

FOLLOWING PAGES:
The Yellowstone River
plunges 308 feet
over the Lower Falls
as it passes through
the 1,200-foot-deep
Grand Canyon of
the Yellowstone.

Crown of the Continent

Hikers scramble to the summit of Reynolds Mountain,
high above a maze of crumbling ridges and ice-scoured valleys
in Montana's Glacier National Park.

I discovered immence ranges of high mountains still to the West of us with their tops partially covered with snow.

Meriwether Lewis

N THE SUMMER OF 1805, Meriwether Lewis scanned a high prairie below the Beaverhead Mountains, a prong of the Bitterroots. The explorer was nearing a pass across the crest of the Rockies in what is now southwestern Montana. Steadying his spyglass, he watched as a horseman, armed with a bow, rode toward him.

Geographic frontiers, created by the upthrust of the Rockies, have created cultural frontiers as well. The Mountain West became the setting for dramatic encounters between the native Indians and exploring parties from Spanish Mexico, British Canada, and finally the expanding United States.

Captain Lewis had taken three men and pushed ahead of the main party, left under the command of co-leader William Clark. Some 15 months earlier, the expedition had

"Let's rodeo!" sounds the announcer's call as cowboy George Eichhorn twirls a lasso in Lincoln, Montana. With his trophy buckle shining, the roper warms up before entering the arena. Throughout the Mountain West, rodeo cowboys demonstrate their skills and compete for prize money.

begun ascending the Missouri River on an epic journey across the continent. The success of their mission now hinged on making contact with Indians who could provide them with horses for a mountain crossing. But the party, sent west by Thomas Jefferson, had not seen an Indian in 1,400 miles.

*N*EARLY TWO CENTURIES LATER, I drive toward the Bitterroots with my wife, Sandy, and our son, Erik. Late spring has taken hold as the green of new grass mixes with darker patches of sagebrush. We follow Horse Prairie Creek as it drains a wide basin divided by a few drift fences. The ground ahead unrolls to the foot of mountains more gentle than the sawtooth peaks farther south. In this corner of Montana, broad valleys wedge apart the ridgetops, letting the big sky pour in.

Somewhere in this expanse, Lewis watched a Shoshone Indian riding forward on a fine horse. Elated by the sight, the captain and his men pushed on, anxious to make friends. But the rider abruptly stopped when he noticed the strangers heading his way. Lewis and his men continued to advance on foot, signaling their peaceful intentions. The Indian, fearing an ambush, backed off to a more secure position.

Lewis laid down his gun and signaled his companions to halt. He walked ahead, holding up a handful of trinkets. One of the men on the flank, unaware of the order to stop, added to the tension by continuing forward. As the captain closed the distance to a hundred paces, the Indian suddenly turned his horse and leaped the creek, disappearing in the willow thickets. Discouraged and still on foot, Lewis and his men trudged ahead, their passage over the mountains still in doubt.

Sandy, Erik, and I turn onto an unpaved road posted with a sign warning that the route to Lemhi Pass is closed. We coast by it, taking our chances. I'm guessing conditions have improved faster than word to remove the sign has filtered down to the road crew. A few miles farther, we pass a second warning sign, not as confidently as we'd passed the first.

The road nudges Trail Creek, winding through fine ranch lands where a cowboy, with a drooping moustache and sagging belly, loads a horse into a trailer. Recently under snow, the dirt road sinks into one mudhole and then another before climbing toward the mountain's saddle. The outflow from a strong spring rushes down the hillside below the ridge.

Captain Lewis paused here to quench his thirst with the "pure and ice-cold water." He thought he had at last realized his dream of reaching the Missouri River headwaters. The party continued to Lemhi Pass above, becoming the first travelers from the United States to straddle the Continental Divide.

Atop the divide, Lewis "discovered immence ranges of high mountains still to the West of us with their tops partially covered with snow."

Sandy, Erik, and I take a last switchback, leveling off at the pass, 7,373 feet in elevation. A sign marks the historic site, and a jackleg fence runs up the ridgeline separating Montana from Idaho. Wildflowers scatter across patches of grass, blooming in whites and yellows as late-season snowbanks fill pockets below the crest of the Beaverheads.

Like a pelt, trees drape the eastern shoulder of the mountain, shredding into patches along the lower edge. On a far hillside, tree-filled gullies angle downslope to merge with creek-side thickets. A knoll bristles with a topknot of pines, and rolling hills dip into hollows. The mountains have reached a balance with the upland prairie—open and forested, high and wide, their bulk strength softened by flowing lines.

Lewis's party descended into present-day Idaho along an Indian trail and the next day made contact with the Shoshone nomads. Lewis completed his mission by acquiring not only their trust but their spare horses as well.

The three of us backtrack the way we came, crossing Horse Prairie and continuing to the ghost town of Bannack. Set on the frontier, the town became a place of sudden reversals—rags to riches, boom to bust. A rich gold strike in 1862 drew thousands of miners and assorted camp followers. In the first year, they extracted minerals worth five million dollars from the banks of Grasshopper Creek. By 1864 the wild boomtown of Bannack had become Montana's first territorial capital.

Bannack now stands empty but not deserted. The residents have left, but a few visitors explore the shell of a town that ended when the gold played out. Bald hillsides curve above historic buildings. Sagebrush crowds the vacant lots between board houses, weathered gray and yellow. Some contain shaky stairways and collapsed floors, but the structures remain surprisingly intact. Protected since the 1950s, the ghost town has been stabilized to prevent further deterioration, but not restored. Park rangers call it "arrested decay."

Inside Skinner's Saloon, I lean on a hardwood bar that has propped up its share of elbows. Dust has settled on an old barber's chair in the corner of what had been the headquarters of a notorious gang. Directed in secret by Henry Plummer, their well-mannered ringleader, the bandits terrorized the region for almost a year and a half. They murdered perhaps a hundred travelers and robbed an unknown number of stagecoaches, freight shipments, and lone horsemen. The outlaws called themselves "The Innocents."

"Henry Plummer and Cyrus Skinner were cellmates at

San Quentin," says Kim Tiplady, a Montana park ranger. "They released Plummer due to his consumption, which they thought was fatal. He came to Bannack looking for gold like everyone else. Bannack being a lawless town to begin with, Plummer saw an opportunity and got himself elected sheriff. He not only was the sheriff, but the leader of the road agents as well."

With the situation growing more desperate, the townspeople formed a vigilante committee pledged to enforce justice, frontier-style. The gallows confession of a gang member implicated Plummer and his cohorts, spurring the committee into action. In short order they tracked down all known gang members, hanging more than two dozen outlaws. The vigilantes left the cryptic numbers "3-7-77" pinned to the bodies of their victims. The symbol, possibly representing the dimensions of a grave—3 feet by 7 feet by 77 inches—continues to appear on the shields of Montana highway patrolmen.

"Sheriff Plummer," Kim adds, "ended up being hung on the same gallows he built for horse thieves."

Faded letters mark the Hotel Meade, a two-story building next to the saloon. Our voices fade and rebound from unexpected directions as the warren of rooms and hallways draws us into separate corners of the hotel.

Originally built as a county courthouse in 1875, the sturdy brick structure became a refuge two years later. Nez Perce Indians, after fighting a pitched battle against soldiers in the Big Hole Valley, fled to Horse Prairie Creek nearby. In Bannack, the women and children of the town barricaded themselves inside the courthouse, and the men built defensive positions in the hills above town. But the expected attack never materialized as the Indians, wanting to avoid a confrontation, made a dash for the uninhabited Yellowstone country.

Leaving the ghost town, we head for the ghost camp of the Nez Perce. The highway takes us into the Big Hole Valley and beyond Wisdom, a small crossroads town. Mountains high enough to hold snow late in the season divide this basin from the Bitterroot Valley to the west. At Big Hole National Battlefield, a footpath emerges from the willows along the river. Following it, we enter the Nez Perce encampment. Weathered gray, the skeletons of more than 50 tepees cluster on a bend of the North Fork of the Big Hole River. Wind blows through each conical framework, carrying flecks of rain. Two ravens, perched on the tips of the tallest poles, suddenly release their grip and let the wind take them. They rise straight up against a line of dark storm clouds edging over the western ridge.

This site was an occasional camp of the Nez Perce, a confederation of bands living where Idaho, Oregon, and

Washington meet. They sometimes paused here on their long journeys to hunt buffalo. In 1877, a year after the Custer defeat on the Little Bighorn, part of the tribe camped by the river on their way east, not for hunting but to escape from soldiers.

Fighting had broken out a few weeks earlier when the Nez Perce were forced to cede ancestral lands and resettle on a smaller reservation. Five bands fled into Montana, seeking refuge in the buffalo country beyond the mountains. Under Chief Looking Glass, they stopped to rest here, confident the soldiers chasing them were lagging far behind. But unknown to the Indians, another military detachment under Colonel John Gibbon had discovered their location. His soldiers moved into position under the cover of darkness.

Catching the Indians by surprise, Gibbon's men fired into the sleeping camp before dawn and charged through a screen of willows. They waded the river and overran half of the village. In the confusion, fleeing women and children were shot down along with the men. Sniper fire by Nez Perce warriors soon halted the attack. Gibbon ordered his men to withdraw to a wooded knoll and dig in. Indian sharpshooters kept them pinned down for more than 24 hours, giving the bands time to break camp and escape.

Victory bought time for the Nez Perce but at a steep price. Between 60 and 90 Indians died in the attack, including some of the best warriors. In the following weeks, the Nez Perce continued to elude their pursuers, winning a series of skirmishes. But after an epic flight of some 1,700 miles, they were intercepted 40 miles from the Canadian border.

"From where the sun now stands," said spokesman Chief Joseph as he concluded his memorable surrender speech, "I will fight no more forever."

Lodge poles bristle against a troubled sky at the Big Hole National Battlefield in southwestern Montana. The tepee frames mark the site where an encampment of Nez Perce Indians, in 1877, defended themselves against an attack by pursuing soldiers of the United States Army.

Next day, eight hikers pile out of cars at the summit of Nez Perce Pass in the Bitterroot Range. The mountains run north and south, falling steeply into the settled valley of the Bitterroot River on one side and the wild Salmon River country on the other.

Dayhikers adjust their packs as trip leader, Cheryl Schoeneman, from the Montana Wilderness Association, points out a few landmarks. The west side of the pass tumbles into Idaho, where a rough road separates the Selway-Bitterroot Wilderness from the Frank Church-River of No Return Wilderness. It's a vast territory of more than 5,700 square miles, an area larger than the state of Connecticut.

Searching among the summits to the west, Cheryl locates Salmon Mountain where she works as a fire lookout, alternating with several other volunteers. As she talks, I notice her license plate. It reads, "I LUV MTS."

The trip leader has lived in Montana for 16 years, but the others are newcomers. They have left behind places as diverse as New York, California, and Oklahoma. "These trips," Cheryl says, "are good for people coming into the area who don't know about it. Some think they can't go into the mountains because of bears. There are no grizzlies in the Bitterroots."

She stoops to help her young friend Andy lighten his pack. He's the most colorfully dressed of the hikers, wearing purple plaid shorts over a pair of blue long johns and a green

Ranchers and hunters, farmers and fishermen find their way to Conover's Trading Post in the crossroads town of Wisdom, Montana. The road to Wisdom runs through the Big Hole Valley—high, wide, and, if not lonesome, at least remote.

sweatshirt. Just turning six years old, Andy will celebrate his birthday this evening. "I'm going to be so tired," he says, "I won't be able to blow out my candles."

The group strings along the trail to Castle Rock, our destination a few miles farther up the ridge. We're following an old Nez Perce route that crosses the mountains. Earlier on the drive to the pass we had stopped at a historic campsite on the valley floor. Old scars marred the trunks of several of the largest ponderosa pines. Ax cuts scored the exposed wood where Indians once peeled off three-foot-long strips of the inner—cambium—layer for food.

Our trail climbs through a thick spire forest, rain-wet and lichen-draped. Weather systems moving across the Pacific Northwest bump into the high Rockies. Deflected upward, moisture-laden clouds cool and unload on the western slopes.

"It sure is great up here," Andy says as the trail levels off. He takes a quick rest before dashing to the front of the line again. The forest thins as we top the ridge. Spring flowers—red penstemons and purple lupines—brighten the open meadows. Yellow blossoms of the glacier lily droop under a light fall of rain. A lens of cloud drifts below, easing over a spur ridge halfway between valley bottom and mountaintop.

We leave the trail at the base of Castle Rock, a square-shouldered volcanic plug. The route to the summit isn't obvious until we've worked around to the side. After a scramble up the eroded face, we stand on top, a windy 7,722 feet in elevation. The ridge divides the West Fork of the Bitterroot to the north from Blue Joint Creek, an area being considered by the forest service for wilderness status. Forested ridges spread in all directions. At this time of year it's a land of green—evergreen and spring green and a dozen shades in between.

A wall of rain draws in from the west, cutting short our stay. We leave the peak, bundled against the downpour. Andy, unable to keep warm, accepts a vest that hangs to his knees and pulls on a long-eared ski cap that slips over his eyes.

As we backtrack to the pass, the sun breaks out. Rain glistens on the leaves of bear grass and huckleberry bushes. A doe, grazing in the open, bolts at our approach, bounding into the forest. Rushing ahead at the end of the walk, Andy spots the parked cars. He gallops down the final length of trail, shouting back, "We made it!"

An hour later, I stop to talk with forest ranger Walt Smith at his home in the Bitterroot Valley. A few months ago he ended his 25-year career as a smoke jumper. A cow skull, with red Christmas-tree balls filling the eye sockets, hangs by the stairs leading to his house. Walt has a rock-gray mustache and a strong Montana handshake.

Cowhands, assisted by paying guests, drive cattle to greener pastures in the Big Belt Mountains. These "city slickers" spend vacation time on a working ranch, experiencing firsthand a cowboy's or cowgirl's way of life.

"One of the incredible things for me," he says, "was being able to jump into some great wilderness." Smoke jumpers are sent to fight fires in terrain too rugged for vehicles to reach. Their work takes them into some of the finest backcountry in the Mountain West and into some of the worst fires.

After parachuting into Yellowstone during the 1988 conflagration, Walt and his crew flew to the Wind Rivers. They jumped into Hole-in-the-Wall Canyon and spread out on both sides of the creek. Driven by fierce winds, the fire made a ridge-to-ridge run. Walt instructed all of his men to keep wearing their helmets and their yellow, fire-retardant shirts as they fought throughout the night to contain the blaze.

"It was just getting sunlight," he says, "and I saw these guys coming down the trail in T-shirts." He strode up, wanting to know why they had disregarded his orders.

"It turned out," he says, "these people were backpackers. They had camped near a beaver pond above. The fire moved so fast, they knew they couldn't outrun it. They jumped into the water and covered their heads with their shirts. They stayed there for an hour and a half as the fire ran over them. It fried everything around them; it burnt everything to the ground."

Wildfire has overtaken Walt a number of times, forcing him to take refuge in burned-over areas. He calls it "going into the black." But fire isn't the only danger smoke jumpers face. "I've had closer calls at night from falling snags and rocks. You're usually in steep terrain where the rocks are black and the ground is black. You can't see them coming. All you hear is 'thump, a-thump, thump,' and you don't know which way to run."

Walt worked as a training foreman at the smoke jumper base in Missoula, where I'm heading next. He says the third or fourth jump is probably the hardest for a rookie. "The first couple of jumps," he tells me, "they're just glad everything worked; they're glad to be alive. Once they get past that, they start thinking about it, thinking about what can go wrong."

Inside the Missoula smoke jumper loft, parachutes hang from the ceiling in colorful panels of blue, white, and yellow. Here veteran smoke jumpers pack and repair their chutes. A poster for the book *Young Men and Fire* hangs on the wall. Author Norman Maclean tells the tragic story of the Mann Gulch fire that took the lives of 13 smoke jumpers in 1949. Down the hallway, a wall plaque honors Don Mackey, a Missoula jumper killed in 1994, one of 14 firefighters who died in the South Canyon fire.

As I read the plaque on the loft wall, a smoke jumper walks past on his way to "the units." This is where the rookies are undergoing the ground phase of their training.

A jump tower, 45 feet tall, rises on the edge of the runway with the Bitterroots forming a backdrop to the south. Instructors have gathered at the foot of the tower, their heads turned upward. A rookie, wearing a padded jumpsuit and blue helmet, braces in the exit door. The spotter, one of two women smoke jumpers at this base, slaps the rookie's leg. He leaps out, head down and body tucked, counting out loud, "One one-thousand, two one-thousand, three one-thousand . . . ."

The cable catches, simulating the shock of an opening parachute, and the rookie jerks and bobs a few times. He continues counting, and at four seconds looks up. On a real jump he would be checking to see if his chute has deployed. All of this is happening as he zips along the cable to the landing platform. Quickly unhooking, he makes a shambling run back to the tower in his heavy gear. The instructors instantly critique his jump and play back a videotape if he has made any mistakes.

Other rookies rappel from a nearby platform to practice tree landings, while another crew runs an obstacle course in heavy boots. At one time the attrition rate for rookies was 50 percent, but fewer candidates now wash out due to better screening and an emphasis on conditioning. After completing about three weeks of training, including at least seven practice jumps, they are ready to parachute into a real fire. Another rookie steps to the door of the tower, preparing to jump.

FOLLOWING PAGES:
In an eastward view from Swiftcurrent Mountain, dawn storm clouds trail a fringe of rain across the high country of Glacier National Park. Plains Indians once entered these mountains to hunt, to gather lodge poles, to fast and pray, and to seek visions.

"The fun never ends at Camp Missoula," an instructor says.

Leaving the smoke jumpers, I head north to the Blackfeet country, east of Glacier National Park. Darrell Kipp, a Blackfeet Indian, meets me at the Red Crow Kitchen in Browning, a small reservation town set in the big open. Plains spread beyond town to break against the high wall of the Rocky Mountains.

"The Blackfeet word for the Rockies means 'the backbone,'" he says. "The word is often translated as 'the backbone of the world.'" Darrell, Ivy League educated but raised in a traditional Indian family, is briefing me on the loss of their mountain lands.

A century ago, he says, the federal government pressured Blackfeet leaders into ceding territory that included much of what became Glacier National Park. "In the Agreement of 1895, the Blackfeet gave up their claim to the

park for 1.5 million dollars. White Calf, a leader at that time, protested. He said, 'The mounains have been my last refuge. We have been driven here and now we are settled.' "

While the Blackfeet spent most of their time on the buffalo plains, they valued the high country. "They went into the mountains," Darrell says, "for functional reasons: for lodge poles, paints, plants—things like that. And they went into the area for spiritual reasons. To identify a sacred site, they might line themselves up with the rising sun where they could look on Chief Mountain in one direction and the Sweetgrass Hills in another. Site selection wasn't random."

Darrell breaks off the conversation to say hello to a friend entering the cafe, a greeting he gives to most of the arriving customers. "My great-grandfather was Chief Heavy Runner," he continues. "He was killed in 1870 when the Second Cavalry massacred his camp while the men were out hunting. They killed 176 people, mostly women and children. My grandfather, just a boy of seven, escaped. Indians back then were clumped in with the trees and the animals. They've begun to restock wolves in Yellowstone," he adds with a slight smile. "I wonder if Glacier Park will restock Indians?"

After graduating with a master's degree from Harvard, Darrell worked for tribal governments throughout the country. But in the late 1970s he came home, feeling the need to return to the place where he grew up. "This is our original homeland. We were put here."

He established the Piegan Institute, refusing to accept government funding, and began surveying the community to determine what traditions remained. He was surprised to learn that only 30 percent of the tribe spoke their own language. "Tribal languages are disappearing everywhere," he says, "and we realized our language was going to die."

Darrell and his colleagues have focused on reviving their native tongue. "Our goal is to have a thousand fluent speakers in ten years," he says. "Language may be the crucial factor in surviving into the next century. And it's a powerful bond to this place. We can look back into the language for our genesis. The stories don't mention a migration. They talk about the rising of consciousness. As far as I'm concerned, we woke up here."

Returning to Montana a month later, I hike into the backcountry of Glacier National Park. I'm breaking the first rule of travel in bear country by walking alone. Approaching Kootenai Lakes, my intended camp, I meet two wide-eyed hikers. They have just come from the lake where they heard a terrifying sound coming from the far shore. It was the cry of a moose calf, they think, being attacked by wolves or perhaps a grizzly. Unable to see, they couldn't be sure. All they could do

Rookie smoke jumpers (opposite) wait to practice parachute landing falls. In a few days these elite firefighters from the Missoula base will make their first jump from an airplane. Aspiring smoke jumper Stephanie Nelson (above) wears a jumpsuit with a high collar that helps to give her protection during landings.

was listen to the cry of the dying animal for five long minutes. The hikers hurry down the trail to report the incident, and I continue to the Kootenais.

A marshy peninsula covers the middle of the largest lake, screening the far shore. No one else is here. At first nothing moves. But soon the head of a beaver breaks the surface with a V-wake trailing behind. It swims back and forth, curious about the two-legged animal on shore. Arching its back, it slips smoothly underwater, swimming with natural grace. But a moment later it surfaces and leaves the water a changed animal. On land the beaver waddles along, its ungainly body burdened by the added weight of gravity.

Before setting up the tent, I check for tracks. Beaver have recently trailed across the shore mud along with deer, moose, and bears—a black bear mother and cub. But I can find no sign of a grizzly or a wolf. As I poke around, a whitetail doe with a soft, russet coat leaves the trees to browse along the shore. It moves with the precise steps of a dance so hypnotic that I watch until the deer drifts back into the trees.

A spire forest rings the lake, and the rock spires of the Citadel Peaks stand silhouetted above them. Soon a cow moose steps from the island brush and enters the lake on spindly legs. Wading belly-deep, the moose sticks its muzzle underwater up to its ears. After browsing the lake bottom, it lifts its head, jaws chewing away on a leafy plant. Another moose, hidden in the willows nearby, snorts. Suddenly, a burst of splashing erupts from behind the island as animals, perhaps wolves, run en masse across the shallows and into the woods.

Before dark, a bull moose joins the other moose, its antlers branching from a body about the size of a couch. It dunks its head completely underwater, walking and feeding for a long moment. Then with a sudden uplift, it breaches the surface as if it just remembered where it is. Both moose appear jumpy, stopping often to stare into the fringe of trees not far from my camp. They finish feeding and slosh out of the water, flinging spray with doglike shakes.

Long after I turn in, the sky holds its light. But it's dark when a heavy crash, sudden and jarring, brings me instantly awake. My body reacts before my consciousness can sort out impressions. A tremendous splash follows as something hits the lake. Bedded down nearby, a doe springs away, startled. A stillness fills the gap left behind as I listen. No sound. I grab the pepper spray, an aerosol can designed to repel bears, and step outside the tent. A lens of silver floats among the trees. Not a ripple stirs the waters of the lake.

Unable to find the source of the noise, I crawl back inside the tent and soon fall asleep. But at dawn I'm up again for an early start. Due to snowdrifts, backcountry rangers have marked "itinerary not recommended" on my permit and have kept the higher camps closed. That means a long day hike to reach Stoney Indian Pass, one of the finest views in the park.

As I heat water, a snowshoe hare appears a few feet away and stops when it realizes it's not alone. It stares in my direction for a puzzled moment before turning around, its long hind feet flashing with each hop.

*H*ANGING MY FOOD HIGH off the ground away from bears and other animals, I turn up the trail toward the pass. Murky light soaks through the tree-shaded gaps where mossy logs sink into moss-carpeted duff. Direct sunlight touches only the tips of the conifers, and undergrowth crowds the path. I weave shoulder-high through rank patches of thimbleberry and cow parsnip, a favorite grizzly snack at this time of year.

"They eat the stalks like celery," said park ranger Dave Casteel yesterday as we walked up the Grinnell Glacier Trail. Above us stood the Garden Wall, a thinly-worn ridge separating two glacier-carved basins. The lean mountaineer, who has worked as a naturalist in the national park since 1965, knows his bears. He pointed out claw marks in the bark of trees where black bears had climbed and showed me the digging scars where a grizzly had flipped patches of turf upside down to eat the glacier lily bulbs. Although he carried a can of bear spray on his hip, he had never used it. "Hey-yaw," the ranger shouted to warn any bears of our approach, "Hey-up!"

Bears in the park have mauled four people this season, an activity Dave called "disciplining." Often they will attack someone who has broken a rule of etiquette, like approaching a sow with cubs or appearing on the trail unannounced. Usually the injuries are minor, and the park rangers will close down the area long enough to let the bear calm down. "Americans are lawbreakers," Dave said. "We're so used to breaking civil laws that we break natural laws too. But you can't feed bears without consequences."

Hikers are advised to avoid surprise encounters with bears by making lots of loud noise. But I feel awkward shouting at each bend of the trail. Instead, I try knocking a couple of stones together. Several whitetails jump off the path when I round a blind curve. But they pause when they hear the clack-clack, clack-clack. Curious to know what's making such a strange sound, they step back to investigate. I toss the rocks away and keep walking.

Where the trail branches, I turn up the slope through stands of alder and ash, passing pocket meadows where stalks of bear grass poke up like candlesticks. The tree cover thins as the trail switchbacks into the high country, revealing the bare crest of the Lewis Range. The waters of Pass Creek cascade down the sedimentary steps. Churned white, the creek fans out on ledges and funnels into chutes cut through the cliffs.

A windswept stand of subalpine fir screens the approach to Stoney Indian Lake. The glacial tarn lies in a cirque routed from the mountain wall. Still in shadows, the lake water is an obsidian green, dark and glassy. Ice slabs crowd the outlet, blown to one side by downslope winds. Banks of unmelted snow angle down to the water's edge and fill a stack of shelves stepping up the face of Wahcheechee Mountain.

I unstrap my ice ax and follow the north shore. The route traverses a drift of snow that drops precipitously into the icy water. But a moose has left a set of tracks in the crust, giving me good footing. Planting the ax point with each step, I cross without trouble, wondering what drew this lone moose toward the pass. Perhaps it only wanted to leave behind the trees and mosquitoes for a wider perspective. The route threads between a cliff wall and the lake before climbing the final ridge to the pass. Rivulets of meltwater braid down the open slopes and tunnel beneath the snowpack.

At Stoney Indian Pass, another world opens. Perched glaciers hang on the face of Cathedral Peak, a high point along the massive escarpment. Sharp-crested ridges, two and three deep, encircle an alpine basin below, and a notched wall frames the farthest peaks, blue with haze. Snowmelt pitches down the facing cliff in linked waterfalls, spilling into Atsina Lake. Its opacity comes from rock flour as fine as talcum powder suspended in the water, scattering light in the blue-green spectrum. Countersunk below sheer-walled summits, the turquoise lake lies surrounded by a vertical wilderness.

Snow has recently melted off the slope where I sit among a yellow cascade of glacier lilies. Birds flitter about while a Columbian ground squirrel chirps nearby. The season has eased into the second half of July, arriving with a burst of life, soft and colorful. But whatever can live here has the tenacity to survive in a harsh, winter-dominated land.

I scan the surrounding cliffs for mountain goats but without luck. Earlier I had watched, with my wife and son, a herd gathered high above the Swiftcurrent Trail. We passed the binoculars back and forth as a dozen white-coated goats grazed and lounged on a grassy bench. Two kids frolicked about as their mother stood guard. A billy eased along a narrow ledge above the others, crossing the crumbling rock with surefooted agility. As we watched, a bald eagle shot above the skyline, wheeled, and disappeared behind the ridge.

Turning back from the pass, I glissade down the steepest snowbank and descend the trail at a fast clip. I have a boat to catch. After covering about eight miles, I reach Goat Haunt. The blue expanse of Waterton Lake, walled by mountains on each flank, spreads to the north. Driftwood, washed down by last month's flood, chokes the shoreline below the ranger station. An excursion boat, the *International*, has docked nearby, ready to return to the north end of the lake, named for the eccentric English naturalist Charles Waterton.

When the pilot blows the horn, I board with the returning passengers. The boat eases away from shore and swings north, following the track of a glacier that once trenched its way through these mountains. Standing in the bow, I lean on the railing and watch the boat's prow slice through water as blue as the color a child would use to paint an imaginary lake.

A voice comes over the intercom to announce that we are crossing the international boundary, the 49th Parallel. We soon pass a ruler-straight swath cut through the forest, running up the mountains on each side of the lake. We have entered Canada and Waterton Lakes National Park. The mountains on one side of the line look no different than those on the other. But crossing a single line has changed the names on the land. The mountains have become the Canadian Rockies.

Rafters run Bone Crusher Rapid on the Flathead River's Middle Fork, as a breaking wave swallows their boat. This whitewater river edges the southwestern boundary of Glacier National Park.

FOLLOWING PAGES: Water tumbles from Idaho's Salmon River Mountains on a fine autumn morning.

JEFF GNASS

146

Hats held off (left) at the Arlee, Montana, rodeo pay tribute to a bull rider who died the year before. At the Lincoln rodeo (below), a contestant readies himself as a rider ends his wild trip.

FOLLOWING PAGES: Bull and rider part company in a swirl of dust.

"Buk-sa-put!" calls the Blackfeet announcer. "Let's go!" To the sound of drumbeats, traditional dancers begin the grand entry at the North American Indian Days pow-wow, held at the foot of the mountains in Browning, Montana.

PRECEDING PAGES: Thousand-foot cliffs of the Chinese Wall follow the Continental Divide and cut across the alpine expanse of Montana's Bob Marshall Wilderness.

*Going-to-the-Sun
Road crosses the
Rockies in Glacier
National Park, passing
below the Garden Wall
(left). To the south, the
glacier-carved horn of
Reynolds Mountain
(above) towers over
the scenic highway.*

*FOLLOWING PAGES:
Crevasse-scarred
Logan Glacier angles
below a razor-edge
divide in the park.*

Northern Reaches

Skiers float across undulating pillows of snow, deep in the Selkirk Mountains of British Columbia. Each winter helicopters fly powder enthusiasts to Canada's remote slopes.

They go on and on and on. They go on forever.

Garnet Clark

BUNDLED SHAPES DISAPPEAR into the falling snow as a line of skiers descends toward the Balfour Hut. We are crossing a glacier high in the Canadian Rockies, but no mountain is visible, no sky can be seen. Thick weather has absorbed all landmarks, leaving no points of reference. Skiing roped together, we find ourselves deep in a whiteout.

We have been on the move for hours, but the interval hardly registers. Arms and legs move in treadmill repetition as the blank surroundings cancel the sensation of forward motion. Our party from the Alpine Club of Canada pushes across the Wapta Icefield, suspended in snow and cloud.

Mountain guide Peter Amann breaks trail at the head of the first rope. He skis with a compass in one hand, setting a course that veers one direction and then another to avoid crevasses and a line of cliffs lying somewhere nearby. At times

Sitting tall in the saddle, Chantal St-Hilaire of the Royal Canadian Mounted Police waters her horse at the Bow River in Banff National Park. Mounties earned a reputation for always getting their man during the Klondike gold rush of the 1890s.

he stops to take a reading from a GPS receiver. Peter has been experimenting with this satellite-linked, global positioning system, testing its usefulness in the high mountains. Despite the instrument's precision, he relies on the compass and his knowledge of the terrain for route finding. Clouds hang still and heavy one moment and stream madly past us the next, adding to the sense of disorientation. The awkwardness of skiing under these conditions increases when skiers are tied together. Each one must keep the length of rope taut, ready to belay anyone who drops into a crevasse in the flat light. As the descent continues, ski poles vibrate in the gusts and the rope bows sideways, carried by a stiff wind.

Lower on Vulture Glacier, the massive prow of a cliff rises dark and smoky above us. Peter recognizes it and takes a quick bearing in case the weather closes in even tighter. Map in hand, he confers with fellow guide Ken Hammell, leading the second rope. They reach a consensus, and we track toward the southeast, topping a rise as the clouds begin to lift.

On a rocky outcrop directly ahead sits the hut, a single point in the expanse of ice and snow now opening before us. With everyone layered under hoods and hats and goggles, expressions are hard to read. I wonder if the others are as surprised as I am. The guides have unerringly led us through the storm.

We are nearing the end of a week-long ski mountaineering trek called the Wapta Traverse. The route crosses a series of interconnected glaciers and ice fields, bordered by high peaks and linked by a series of passes. Following close to the Continental Divide, we began on the Peyto Glacier to the north and will end the journey at Kicking Horse Pass farther south. If the weather clears by morning, we'll cross the divide, leaving Alberta's Banff National Park and entering Yoho National Park in British Columbia. It's early April but no one is thinking spring.

Our traverse began five days ago in unsettled weather. A few snowflakes textured the air as we skied in from the Icefields Parkway and regrouped on the frozen surface of Peyto Lake. I remember Peter studying the low clouds, snagging on the peaks above. "Clag," he called it, using a word that sounded more like a Nordic curse than a comment on the weather.

"Is it usually like this?" I asked.

"The weather isn't usually anything," he said.

"Except arbitrary," Ken added. He snapped his fingers. "It can change like that."

Both guides have learned to keep an eye on the weather. Peter works as an avalanche control officer, and Ken spends his winter months leading heli-ski trips. For me, paying attention to the weather is the first step in coming to terms with an unfamiliar place. By entering these mountains I had put myself in a situation where I was essentially a beginner again, where nothing could be taken for granted. I did this for a chance to spend a few days amid the beauty of the high ice fields. And I did this to experience the glacial conditions that had shaped the profile of the Rockies. I had come to see mountains under the grind of ice.

*O*N THAT FIRST DAY, we passed through the narrows at the end of the lake, leaving behind the valley for the high country above. We attached our climbing skins and began the ascent to the Peyto Glacier. The route followed a steep moraine where, in 1994, an avalanche caught a party of skiers who had camped in the wrong spot. Peyto Peak, banded in rough-cut layers, towered above us.

As we climbed, spindrift avalanches sloughed off the ledges at regular intervals. The largest boomed down the cliff with the sound of distant thunder, but our route of travel lay far enough away not to be threatened. As a precaution, all of us had activated our avalanche transceivers. This device emits a signal that searchers can use to pinpoint the wearer, even if buried under a snowslide. It also can be switched to the receive mode when searching for a victim.

Where the moraine crested in a steep ridge, we removed our skis and walked, using the slow dirge-step of the mountaineer—kick-step, pause, kick-step again. At the toe of the glacier we strapped into climbing harnesses and roped together. In winter, crevasses lie hidden under the snow, difficult to detect. As we ascended, a sheer wall of blue ice, exposed above, gave the only hint that we were on a glacier.

Crossing the headwall, we reached the Wapta Icefield and a beauty I had never seen before. The surface undulated in a whiteness of snow and sky, a whiteness that took hold of the heart. Even the encircling mountains lay shrouded under a thick blanket of snow and ice. Only a few crags and cliffs remained unburied, ripping through the cover in raw outcrops. We were entering a world still emerging from the Ice Age.

"Sometimes," Peter said, "you look around and wonder, 'Where are the mastodons?' "

Weighted under a heavy pack, he continued to break trail, leading the line of skiers in a wide arc to avoid buried crevasses on the edge of an icefall. Looking back, I could trace our narrow track, curving into the blank expanse, trailing away to nothing.

Eight of us crowded inside Peyto Hut, tossing packs on the bunks to claim spaces for the night. Wall-to-wall sleeping platforms, built on two levels, filled one side of the single room and a long counter ran down the other. That evening we cooked dinner on a two-burner camp stove. The accommodations were spartan, but considering the alternatives of a tent or snow cave, very comfortable.

Years ago Peter spent a cold night on the Columbia Icefield when an unexpected storm overtook him and his companions. It was an experience that led to his becoming a guide. They had gone up for the day but had to bivouac without sleeping bags when the weather prevented their return. After building an igloo, they spent the night walking in a circle to stay warm. "That's when I decided," he said, "to learn how to get around in these mountains."

Next morning, we divided into two groups to practice crevasse rescue and avalanche searches. Taking turns, we rigged ropes and pulled each other up a cliff face to simulate a crevasse wall. Each of us then had to locate a transceiver hidden under the snow by walking a search pattern using our own instrument. Knowing we might need these skills in the days ahead gave the lessons an immediacy not often found in a classroom. The guides took the training seriously; both have had to extract companions from crevasses or dig out those buried under avalanches. After 20 years in the mountains, Peter had come to understand the unpredictable nature of this terrain. "An avalanche," Peter said, "doesn't know you're an expert. These mountains don't care who you are or what you know."

That afternoon the weather cleared enough for us to ascend the col between North Rhondda and Mount Baker. We

Mount Rhondda rises from the Wapta Icefield high in Banff's Waputik Mountains. Snow has melted from the lower glaciers, exposing an area of sinuous moraines and fractured ice crossed by the author during a winter ski traverse.

spread out in a line for safety and skied up the flowing contours of the glacier. Snowfields rolled into pure white dunes and dipped in windswept scoops. Ken pointed to the east face of Baker where a wide slab had broken free during the night and avalanched down the mountainside. A vague line of shading creased the snowfield ahead. I was surprised to learn it was a crevasse. When entering a new environment, the slight variations that can make a critical difference aren't always obvious. As we gained height, the horizon widened to reveal a great circle of mountains.

Sunlight broke through the clouds like the eye of a sleeper trying to open. It flickered for a moment and then closed as snow showered down and gusts stirred the air. At the pass, the wind raked across the divide, blowing gale force. We turned back to the hut without delay, gliding down through deep powder, linking turns. Mary Krupa, from Alberta, shouted back, "It's the closest thing to being on a cloud, eh?"

Next morning, Peter announced that a large pressure drop had occurred during the night. He expected a cold front to hang around for several days. "Cheer up," he told us, "things will get worse."

Visibility outside the hut was low as blowing snow spiked the air. With each pulse of wind came a momentary whiteout. As we roped up, Ken walked down the line checking to make sure everyone had turned on their avalanche beepers. We shuffled toward the next hut, using climbing skins on the steepest incline. Looking back from a wide col, Peyto Hut appeared to be a single rock lost in a vast snowscape.

Our route contoured along an ice-capped escarpment above the headwaters of the Bow River, whose principal source is glacial meltwater. At times the clouds thinned, letting a pale arctic light filter through. Snow whirled and tangled in wild tendrils along the ridgeline. It felt good to be here.

We unroped and skied below the snaggletooth of St. Nicholas Peak. Bow Hut lay somewhere downhill. Trying to balance backpacks, we descended a steep pitch in near-whiteout conditions. The visual field flattened into two dimensions, making it difficult to judge the degree of slope. Crusted snow switched unexpectedly to pockets of deep powder. I felt myself tensing up, unwilling to give in to the tug of gravity. After a few spills, I reached our destination.

Bow Hut had the reputation of being the Hilton of the ice-field shelters. It was the only one with sleeping quarters separate from the kitchen and it had the added luxury of a woodstove for heat. That night and the next we shared the hut with another ski mountaineering party doing the traverse in the opposite direction, from south to north.

FOLLOWING PAGES: Dwarfed by a massive wall of ice, a group of mountaineers crosses a shoulder of Vowell Glacier in the Purcell Mountains. As it moves imperceptibly, the glacier breaks into deep crevasses that result from areas of ice moving at speeds different from the pace of surrounding areas.

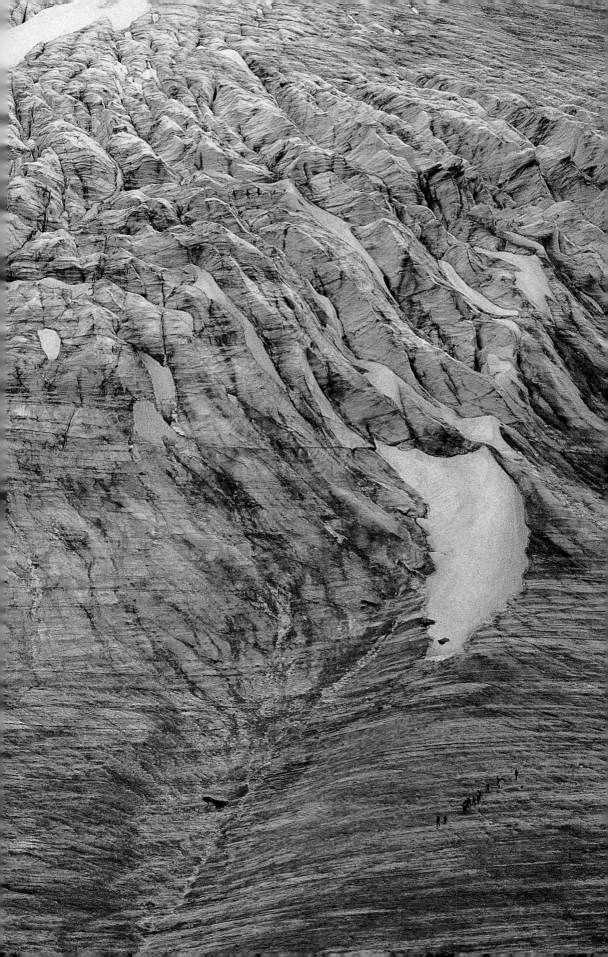

Taking advantage of a break in the weather, we took off the next day for a ski ascent of Mount Gordon. From the summit a few hours later, we could see most of the ice field. Jagged outcrops broke above the smooth curves of snow and the tree-filled valleys far below. Ice-carved crags clustered to the south.

"They go on and on and on," said Garnet Clark from British Columbia. He looked out on mountains reaching to every horizon. "They go on forever."

We turned back to the hut after making a second ascent of nearby Mount Rhondda. The line of skiers descended as a halo circled the sun, hinting of a change in weather. That night the clouds closed in, bringing more snow. The fresh accumulations triggered a number of minor avalanches, visible the next morning. Their run-out paths radiated below an icefall across the amphitheater from the shelter. As we packed up for the trek to the Balfour Hut, Peter gave us his daily weather forecast.

"There's good days and there's bad days," he said. "And then there are mountain days—cheer up, it will only get worse." No one argued with him. That afternoon we descended Vulture Glacier in a total whiteout.

*N*OW, AS WE REACH the Balfour Hut late on the fifth day, we unclip from the ropes. We are getting used to skiing under adverse conditions; the past days on the ice field have been good conditioning. But tomorrow's crossing of the high col might depend more on luck than preparation.

Before the ropes can be coiled, drifting snow has covered our tracks behind us. We stomp our boots and enter. Garnet, still wearing his body harness, places a bucket of snow on the camp stove to melt for water. His gray beard keeps its frosted look even after he's shaken off the snow. Mary finds a place to rest on the bunk. Although tired, her spirits remain high. She began planning this trip last year and didn't waver when she became pregnant six months ago. "Out there today," she says, "I began to think maybe I shouldn't be doing this."

Wind continues to kick up outside. Peter shuts the door behind him as a cloud of steam rolls into the hut, cold air meeting warm. After making sure everyone's present, the guide outlines our situation. Tomorrow we face the most dangerous leg of the trip, a four-and-a-half-hour ascent of the Balfour High Col. To reach this pass, the group will ski along a ramp on the east face of Mount Balfour, passing below a high-frequency icefall. Once clear of that hazard, we will skirt crevasses and snow-loaded slopes on the way to the summit. Visibility will be critical. "If the weather's bad," he tells us, "we can't go on. We'll have to return to Bow Hut and exit there."

For a moment no one responds. Turning back would mean leaving the traverse uncompleted. Whatever decision the guides make we'll support, but Garnet speaks up from the corner of the hut. "We want to go on," he says.

Through the window, I study Mount Balfour across an intervening moraine. Blankets of snow smother the heights with only a scatter of rocky outcrops breaking the surface. Wind-loaded slopes slant upward, climbing into the clouds. Peter points out the ramp we'll take on the approach. It angles below a wall, weighted under a massive layer of crumbling, blue ice. Even from a distance it looks threatening.

A full moon rises behind a scrim of clouds as the rumble of an avalanche carries up from a lower, unseen slope. Several times during the day, a layer of snow had settled under us with an ominous "whompff." "New snow instability," Ken called it. Nothing is certain as the day closes.

Before turning in, I take a final look at tomorrow's route. Clouds have moved in, hiding the summit. On the snowfield leading to the ramp, wind has carved the surface in a sinuous, rippling pattern. I can detect the mass of ice, balanced on the edge of the cliff. The hanging glacier has a beauty that can suddenly give way in an avalanche of snow and ice.

After a night spent in the Balfour Hut, the guides face a decision. Whether we attempt to cross the pass or turn back hinges on the weather. In the early light, our chances of continuing the traverse don't look good. A thick cloud cover obscures the route. Winds are driving the snow sideways.

"How's the weather?" Mary asks.

"Horizontal," I tell her.

But after breakfast the wind dies down, and the guides step outside to talk. Peter smokes his pipe and Ken studies the sky. When they finish their discussion, Ken strides into the hut, energized. "We're going," he tells us. "Get packed up." Everyone clicks into motion at once, trying not to collide with others in the tight quarters. Ken ties a bundle of wands onto his pack. These can be placed in the snow to mark our course. If we are caught in a whiteout during the long ascent, we'll need them to find our way back to the hut.

Again Peter breaks trail. New-fallen snow lies in thick cushions on the old. Nearing the icefall, we pause, taking our last chance to rest before entering the danger zone. From here on we won't be able to stop until clear of the hanging glacier.

After checking gear, we begin the passage. The roped teams move beneath the icefall, skiing steadily. House-size chunks balance above us, threatening to topple without warning. The ice moves imperceptibly. When it reaches the brink of

FOLLOWING PAGES: Evening light strikes the rugged face of the Cathedral Crags, a landmark in Yoho National Park. The crags are typical of some ranges in this part of the Rockies, where limestone erodes into castle-like formations.

the cliff, it breaks into immense blocks and pinnacles called seracs that at some unpredictable moment will crash onto the ramp below. As soon as we enter the icefall, sunlight breaks through a chink in the clouds, illuminating our route. We pass below the serac wall where fragments of recently fallen ice lie covered by last night's snow. As we continue to ascend, the patch of light stays with us. Our luck holds.

The lead guide takes a zigzag course to avoid the most hazardous terrain, threading between open crevasses and potential avalanche slopes. A large split in the ice, about a dozen feet wide, has opened nearby. The last time the guides crossed the pass it wasn't here. The crevasse drops into the blue depths of the glacier with snow overhanging the lip. The grade lessens as we near the summit of the pass and the direct sunlight fades, having escorted us beyond the icefall.

Topping the high col, we pass through a field of diffused light, a luminous mist suspended in midair. We ski down the far side on a rolling plain of untracked snow—we have crossed the Continental Divide. We now find ourselves on the Waputik Icefield, bordered by a sawtooth ridge that guides us to our next hut on a spur of Mount Daly. The sides of the mountain, heavy with new snow, flare up on each side of the shelter. To avoid the unstable slopes, Peter leads us along a narrow ledge where we take off our skis. As he belays from above, we climb up, one by one, punching handholds into the wall of snow.

An early wake-up comes on the last morning. The frosted windows make it hard to guess the weather. Although not as dangerous as the high col, today's terrain may prove to be more difficult. We will descend 4,000 feet from the ice field to the Trans-Canada Highway at Kicking Horse Pass. The route drops down sheer slopes, makes a twisting run through a canyon, and crosses a frozen waterfall. And that's only the top half.

I step outside. Lowering clouds move uneasily, bringing with them a feeling of early winter. I have to remind myself it's April. We ski toward Niles Pass under a chalk-white sky.

Conditions deteriorate and skiing becomes more difficult in the gray half-light. We angle to one side of a peak. Ahead, the route follows a long traverse beneath the east face of Mount Niles. A huge cornice, resting on a ledge of blue ice, caps the peak. The glacier perches above a broad, avalanche-prone slope we have to cross.

Peter skis ahead to set the track and is soon swallowed by the expanse. Once Peter has safely crossed, Ken sends us ahead one by one. He waits until the first skier is halfway across before letting the next begin. We are skiing far apart to lessen the chance of an avalanche taking more than one or two of us. I stand ready, waiting for Ken to give the word.

"Okay Scott," he says calmly, "you can start. Move quickly and don't stop." I ski with a steady kick and glide, glancing up once or twice at the great wall of rock and ice towering above. The last two cross the slope behind me with Ken bringing up the rear.

After everyone has gathered on the far side, Peter sets the course for a steep descent into the valley. We swing left and right, plunging back and forth in a long corkscrew. Soon we drop below tree line. The snow softens. The air has grown warmer and thick with the fragrance of spruce and fir, the first trees we've encountered in a week. After the open ice fields, the forest crowds in, leaving me cut off from the wider sky.

Our party strings out as we pinball through the turns of a ravine. Only after descending the face of the waterfall, frozen and mounded with snow, do I realize what it is. We reach the upper valley faster than anticipated. Mary, worried at the start, has made it down without a serious fall. After removing layers of clothing, we press on.

Wet snow sticks to the skis as we cross Sherbrooke Lake, but conditions turn slippery back in the trees. The final 700 feet drop down a twisting trail filled at a slant with hard-packed snow. Most of the course has to be side-slipped, making the skiing more awkward than on the open slopes above.

Even before catching sight of the highway, I can hear the rumble of trucks below. The rhythms are changing; the pace quickens. As we reach the parking lot, the Wapta Traverse

Glacial meltwater collects in Lake Louise below the towering peaks of the Bow Range. At the lakeside stands Chateau Lake Louise, one of the grand hotels built by the Canadian Pacific Railway to draw tourists to the spectacular scenery of the Rocky Mountains.

is suddenly over. My jaw unclenches; the grip on the poles relaxes. I don't feel I've arrived as much as landed. After a week in the clouds, I've touched ground.

Next time I set foot on a glacier, the snow has melted and the crowds have gathered. It's midsummer. On this particular day, seven snow coaches have parked on the surface of Athabasca Glacier in Jasper National Park. The glacier flows from the Columbia Icefield above, a vast sheet covering 120 square miles. Lying among the high peaks on the Great Divide, the ice field is the largest in the Rocky Mountains. Tourists by the hundreds mill about with fixed grins, documenting their presence with camera and camcorder. They come from places as diverse as the western rim of the Pacific and northern Europe, from eastern Canada and the southern United States. Some keep close to the coaches, content just to stand on an actual glacier. Others venture a short way, taking small, tentative steps, unsure of their footing on ice a thousand feet thick.

This dense tongue of ice flows down the outlet valley at a mid-glacier rate of 264 feet a year. But even on the move, its mass continues to shrink. Since the first recorded sighting in 1898, the glacier has been melting back faster than the winter snows are compressed into new ice.

Streaked by dust and fallen debris, a smaller glacier hangs on the face of Mount Andromeda to the south. To the north, a spur of the Snow Dome sweeps above the valley with its ice-capped summit forming a rare triple divide. From this single feature, the hydrographic apex of the continent, meltwater flows into three oceans.

Runnels score the surface of the glacier where I stand. They tumble downslope to join the Athabasca drainage, eventually reaching the Arctic Ocean by way of the MacKenzie River. To make the Pacific connection, meltwater drains through the Columbia River system. The Snow Dome completes the triple split by sending glacial water toward the Atlantic through rivers that empty into Hudson Bay.

Another claim for a three-ocean divide has been made for Triple Divide Peak in Montana. Runoff from the rocky prominence flows into the Pacific, into the Atlantic, and into Hudson Bay. "The crux of the problem," says park warden Greg Horne, "is whether you consider Hudson Bay part of the Arctic Ocean or part of the Atlantic."

He points out that the bay's tidal exchanges occur through a deep strait connected to the Atlantic and not through the shallow channels linking it with the Arctic Ocean. "Based on ocean currents, Hudson Bay is part of the Atlantic. That makes the Snow Dome the only point in North America dividing three oceans."

When the horn honks, passengers scurry back to the

snow coach. Before leaving, I bend down and take a drink of glacier water. The taste is as cold and pure as the stiff breeze sweeping down from the ice field.

Turning back, the driver follows a fixed route across the ice and up the steep wall of the flanking moraine. The coach, designed to operate in six-wheel drive, inches up the grade on low-pressure, oversize tires. Transferring to a bus on top, the passengers return to the Icefields Parkway on a road overlooking Sunwapta Lake. The lake has formed at the toe of the glacier, collecting meltwater that fell as snow 200 years ago. It releases the overflow into the Sunwapta River, a tributary of the Athabasca River.

On another branch of the Athabasca the next day, boatman RJ Kingston sits in the stern of his raft, gripping a pair of oars. "Paddle forward," he calls to the passengers in front.

We dip our blades and pull as the current picks up speed and RJ steers for the deepest channel. Waves splash on board as the raft begins an eight-mile descent of the Maligne, a

Cameras click and whir as onlookers gather on the shore of Jasper National Park's Maligne Lake—the largest natural lake in the Canadian Rockies. A moose wades in to feed on succulent water plants.

fast river dropping an average 66 feet a mile. In case of a spill, each passenger wears a wet suit under a fleece pullover and spray jacket, itself worn beneath a life jacket. A helmet caps the ensemble. On alpine rivers you dress for failure.

Dashing headlong through the rapids of Miracle Mile, we enter a stretch of broken water without let-up. The river offers a continuous run of white water. Sunshine glints off the waves as the raft rounds a bend.

Historians attribute the naming of the Maligne to Father Pierre Jean de Smet, a Jesuit missionary who traveled through this region in 1846. When his party reached the mouth of the waterway and had a difficult crossing, he called it the "wicked river." I might call it worse, if I had to take a dunking in these icy waters without a wet suit.

This river valley in Jasper National Park has long held a reputation for being different, even mysterious. During fall and winter the Maligne becomes a lost river, sinking below the surface. Its flow disappears into Medicine Lake before emerging more than ten miles away. When not charged by the summer runoff, even Medicine Lake dries up, draining through subterranean channels in the limestone bedrock. The Maligne system is one of the largest sinking rivers in the world.

Brian Young, a river guide born in Jasper, has his own name for the region. "We call it," he says, " 'the valley of terminally bad weather.' " Today must be an exception. Full sunlight falls on the water as Brian stands up in the raft ahead to scout the rapids. With a couple of strokes, our boatman catches an eddy behind a submerged boulder. Seated at the rear of the raft, RJ pivots the bow to dodge and weave through the rocky channel. Our flotilla of three boats rides the flowing corridor, threading between forest walls. Cathedral spires of spruce and lodgepole pine rise from the river's edge where the roots of dwarf evergreens grip a mossy boulder.

Suddenly we come upon a great bull elk, reclining on a bed of green moss next to the river. Sunlight warms his wide-spreading antlers, filtering through the velvet in a soft nimbus. The forest monarch watches us closely, alert but without fear, as the current pulls us quickly downriver.

After sluicing through the Squeeze, we reach the pullout and derig the boats. The river continues to flow, moving fast and steady on its journey into the far north.

SMOKE FILTERS through the trees ahead, rising in a faint column above the boreal forest. "That's their camp," says Marianna Keller, pointing to the drift of smoke. "It looks like someone is home." We have been walking for a couple of hours along a glacier-fed river in the mountains of northern British Columbia. I have teamed up with photographer Paul Chesley to search for a family of nomadic hunters called the MacDonald Indians. Marianna, who left Switzerland to live in the wilds of Canada, has met members of the small band before. She will try introducing us to them, but the Indians don't speak English, and locals say no outsider has been able to understand their native dialect.

Rain tapers off as clouds drift down the mountainside and break apart in smoky patches. To the north, the Terminal Range shoulders above the pale blue river, pushing beyond the trees into alpine tundra and stark summits. We've entered the northern reaches of the Rockies, the final mountains of the great continental chain.

Even in midsummer the coolness of the day hints of winter. We are farther north than I first realized. When darkness didn't come until midnight and dawn only a few hours later, I checked the map. This country lies at the same latitude as Glacier Bay on the coast, farther north than Juneau, Alaska.

We are hiking up an abandoned mine road. We've already passed the site of a deserted camp used by the Indians last spring. With growing anticipation, we now approach a cluster of tents pitched among the dark spruce trees. A whiff of wood smoke drifts our way.

Suddenly the woods erupt in a furor of barking. Half a dozen dogs, ringing the perimeter of the camp, noisily warn of our arrival. Ron Mearow, a white-haired trapper who has lived with the MacDonald Indians for several years, steps into the trail. Quieting the dogs, he recognizes Marianna in her yellow slicker, and invites us in to Nine-mile Camp.

The trapper doesn't speak the language of his Indian friends, but communicates with hand signs. He introduces us to Rosie and Maggie, both in their 60s, and to their older brother Walter. Wearing carefully patched clothes slick with animal fat, the Indians greet us with shy smiles. All three are thin and have difficulty hearing. They never married. None of them have children. Two other members of the band are living higher in the mountains at another camp.

Wall tents, fastened to spruce poles lashed together, stand to one side of the central fire. Tarps have been rigged above them to shed the heaviest rains. Next to the campfire, supplies lie piled on a bed of spruce boughs. Unsplit rounds of aspen and spruce smolder next to a drying rack. Slabs of meat, cut to a translucent thinness, drape down from a log scaffold.

Weaving through the hanging meat, I dodge blackened chunks of moose and Stone sheep, a variety related to the Dall sheep found farther north. Massive leg bones, saved for the marrow, dangle next to thin strips of sinew and globs of fat.

Nothing is wasted. The blue-eyed trapper tears off a shred of jerky and hands it to me.

As I chew on a smoky piece, and keep chewing to work it soft enough to swallow, the strangeness of all of this hits. We have arrived in a camp of nomadic hunters where language fails us, in mountains unknown to us but home to them. The tang of wood smoke and curing meat surrounds us, permeating the campsite in layered scents reaching deep into the human past. Trace your roots back far enough and this is where they lead—to a camp deep in the forest, strung with drying meat.

Often the scent of a fresh kill, Ron says, will draw bears and wolves to their camp. The dogs, each with its own shelter, act as a trip wire to guard against them. Bear Dog, stoutly built with a neck thicker than his head, looks like he could take on a grizzly. "But he's scared of bears," the trapper says, and panics whenever one appears. "I keep a 12-gauge at the head of the bed with two slugs chambered. You never know when a cranky ol' grizzly might come around at night."

Maggie, hands knotted with arthritis, lights a pile of twigs in a pan beneath the meat. As smoke billows up and ashes drift down like snow, she takes me aside. The Indian woman rummages in a pack and brings out a photo of her dogs when they were puppies. She tells me about them, talking on and on in a language that has closed in upon itself, a language unable to take her beyond the circle of her brothers and sisters.

On the edge of camp, Rosie returns to the hide of a bull moose, stretched on a tilted frame. She was working on it when we arrived. Using a metal-tipped tool, she scrapes the fur from the skin with a steady, repetitious motion. She'll have it ready for tanning by tomorrow evening and eventually will use the leather for sewing moccasins and mukluks.

Based deep in the mountains, the MacDonald Indians move with the seasons, stopping at set camps along the river. They settle into log cabins during the deep of winter but find them too confining. At the first opportunity in spring, they return to the open camps. The Indians once used dogs to pack their gear and pull toboggans. Now they drive a pair of four-wheel, all-terrain vehicles, using the old road to reach their other camps. They have selected technology to fit their nomadic lifestyle, living at the close of the 20th century much as their family lived at its start.

No one I talked to knew the origins of this hunting band. Ron thinks they might be related to the Beaver Indians, an Athapaskan group living farther south. But adding to the mystery, he has heard they originally came from somewhere to the north more than a century ago. Their father, Charlie

MacDonald, guided military survey parties through these mountains when the Alaska Highway was built in 1942. "They were living here before the highway ever thought of going through," Ron says.

After spending a couple of hours at Nine-mile Camp, we say goodbye. Each of the Indians gives us a gentle handshake as things draw to a close. Following the river back, we leave behind the last of the MacDonald Indians.

In the forests of northern British Columbia, trapper Ron Mearow (left) lives with the MacDonald Indians, a small band of nomadic hunters. Maggie MacDonald prepares moose jerky at their camp.

"It doesn't look good," says bush pilot Urs Schildknecht the next morning. He hands us a weather report he just received by fax. Outside, the clouds have thickened and settled over the higher ridges. Wind chops the surface of the lake into white scales. Paul and I are staying at the pilot's lodge on Muncho Lake, doing what seasoned travelers in the north country take for granted. We are waiting for the weather to break.

After leaving the MacDonald Indians we drove north on the Alaska Highway along Muncho Lake. Running for more than seven miles between the Terminal and Sentinel ranges, the lake forms the core of a provincial park. Three other provincial parks lie in northern British Columbia. The Alaska Highway links Stone Mountain with Liard River Hot Springs, but the distant Kwadacha is reached only by floatplane or a long trek by horse or foot.

Urs, a Swiss Canadian, regularly flies fishermen into remote lakes in his plane, a powerful radial-engine Beaver mounted with floats. He has come to know this country well. "But only from the air," he says. These northernmost Rockies enclose a region of high peaks and deep solitude, a region few know from the ground.

Walking along the lakeshore, I climb a knoll. On the east, ridges carve through the clouds in steeply angled strata, raw and mostly treeless. Summer runoff floods down the barren uplands, funneling through ravines and spreading out in broad alluvial fans. On the west side of the lake, a transient green covers the slopes with only the higher summits nudging above the trees. This country lies under snow more months of the year than it remains snow-free. Within a few weeks the first snows will arrive to dust the mountains.

The Terminal Range trails into the clouds, and the day drifts into the long summer twilight of the subarctic. Grounded and running out of time, I decide to find a route into the mountains on foot. Driving farther north, I round a bend. Several mountain caribou stand on the highway shoulder, licking the remnants of last winter's road salt. They are a reminder of how far north the Rockies have pushed. As a truck approaches, the caribou dash into the brush with their splayed hoofs, adapted for crossing snow and muskeg, slapping the ground. A logging truck motors past, loaded with white spruce for the chopstick factory in Fort Nelson.

Approaching the northern end of the Terminal Range, I leave the car behind and enter the wet green of the taiga. I head toward a spur ridge, weaving through black spruce. They clump together in a marshy lowland with a scatter of alder and willow adding to the thicket. A bear would feel right at home in this cover. I search my pack for the pepper spray, but can't find it. The choice is either to return to the lodge or start talking to the bears. Angling up the mountainside, I call out "Hey-up, hey-yah."

White spruce and subalpine fir trail up the steep incline. As I move higher, the trees thin and give way to alpine tundra and then to bare rock. Rain falls and eases off and falls again so lightly I no longer notice it. Across the river, clouds soften the stark lines of the Sentinels, drifting down the folds of the range as gently as sleep descends. Directly above me, a cloud mass balances on the ridge, clinging only to the north side of the crest.

Throughout my travels in the Rockies, I've rarely found mountains without clouds. At times I can't tell where one begins and the other ends. Mountains erode into rumpled masses; clouds build into craggy shapes. One is formed by moisture rising and the other shaped by moisture falling. Mountains give rise to clouds, and clouds wear down mountains in an endless cycle.

Glancing up to check the route, I spot a pair of Stone sheep. A ewe stands close to a lamb on a rocky incline just below the clouds. They face toward me, gray trim under white muzzles and the black horns of the mother curving back. The sheep turn aside without haste and pick their way over the edge, dropping out of sight.

Even at this elevation I'm unable to get a clear view north, so I continue higher. A sheep trail leads up the cut ridge. Entering the clouds, I go only a short distance and stop. The visual field has narrowed to about 20 feet. As I take a drink of water, a slight breeze stirs the clouds around me. And a moment later they part, opening a window to the north.

Rain clouds gather above the farthest reaches of the Terminal Range. Folds of cloud hang above folds of mountain. Cross spurs lift one behind the other into the far distance where the central ridge drops off abruptly. That's where the Liard must lie, marking the end of the Rockies. The path of the river intersects the head of the range at right angles, cutting across the grain of the high country. The clouds stir again, swallowing the last of the mountains.

As I turn back to descend, the perspective shifts. From here, the backbone of North America no longer stretches north but south. It tracks across western Canada and the United States, running between the Liard River and the Pecos, between the Alaska Highway and the Santa Fe Trail, between the subarctic and the American Southwest. The great dividing range connects boomtown and ghost town, national park and open-pit mine, ski slope and sacred mountain. Facing south, I find myself once again at the beginning of the Rockies.

FOLLOWING PAGES: Ready for paddlers, a colorful array of canoes fans out from a dock on Moraine Lake in Banff National Park. Above the smooth lake water at the head of the valley rise some of the dramatic Ten Peaks.

Mountain guide Jocelyn Lang leads a party of hikers high above tree line in the glaciated wilderness of the Purcell Mountains. Later, a helicopter hovers overhead, ready to transport the group to a new location. Heli-hiking has grown in popularity as a summer counterpart to heli-skiing.

FOLLOWING PAGES: Wolf-tooth spires of the Bugaboos cut sharply above ice-mantled mountains on the western flanks of the Rockies.

*Prismatic colors
scatter in the mist of
Takakkaw Falls, leap-
ing over a cliff in a
total drop of 833 feet.
Its name comes from
a Cree word for "It is
wonderful." To the
southwest, also in
Yoho National Park,
lie the still waters of
Emerald Lake.*

Banff tourists gather above milky colored Peyto Lake. Charged with fine

particles of glacial rock flour, the water reflects the blue-green spectrum of light.

Heli-skiers carve
through fresh powder
(above) in the remote
Selkirk Mountains
of British Columbia.
Lifted by chopper
from one ski run to
another, downhillers
can descend 100,000
vertical feet or more
in an action-packed
week of skiing.

Outfitter Wald Olson, with his son Wade (left), packs into Jasper National Park's Tonquin Valley. At the end of the day, the horses eat first (right).

FOLLOWING PAGES: Glacial ice continues to carve the spine of the continent in northern British Columbia at the end of the Canadian Rockies.

Index

Boldface indicates illustrations.

Notes on the Author and Photographer

A resident of Flagstaff, Arizona, author **Scott Thybony** brings to his writing a background in anthropology, a zest for remote places, and experience as a wilderness guide. Scott has written numerous books, trail guides, and articles in national magazines. He is the author of the Society's *Canyon Country Parklands,* and has contributed to many other Society publications.

Paul Chesley, who lives in the Rocky Mountains, in Aspen, Colorado, has been a free-lance photographer with the National Geographic Society since 1975, and has completed more than 35 assignments for the Society. Paul says that he enjoys capturing the lives and cultures of people in places such as Australia, Bhutan, Japan, Norway, Iceland, France, Canada, and the United States.

Acknowledgments

The Book Division wishes to thank the individuals, groups, and organizations named or quoted in the text for their help in the preparation of this volume. In addition, we are grateful for the assistance of the following: Aspen Ski Co., Anthony Atwell, Brewster Transportation, Lisa Bringardner, Ron Britton, Canadian Mountain Holidays, Inc., Cloud Eagle, Sue Dorame, Curtis Featherston, Brenton Gardner-Smith, Glenna Goodacre, Verdean Heinier, Vinca Hougen, Robert Jenkins, Billy Kidd, Annie Kuhles, Carole Lee, Ramon J. Lopez, Bobby Lujan, Skip Miller, Valery Moore, Norad, Frank Ohlin, Philip Paul, Brian Ratcliffe, Rick Richardson, David Rigsby, Mike Shim-Konis, David Swersky, Mike Taylor, Hunter Thompson, Sandy Thybony, Doreen VanAsten, Martin von Neudegg, Brady Ward, Franki Webster, Tony Williams, Chris and Jerome Young.

Additional Reading

Readers may wish to consult the *National Geographic Index* for related articles. The following may also be of interest: Audrey Benedict, *The Southern Rockies;* Bernard De Voto, ed., *The Journals of Lewis and Clark;* Jerry Camarillo Dunn, Jr., *The Rocky Mountain States;* Ben Gadd, *Handbook of the Canadian Rockies;* John McPhee, *Rising From the Plains;* Graeme Pole, *Canadian Rockies;* Jeremy Schmidt, *Adventuring in the Rockies;* Tom J. Ulrich, *Mammals of the Northern Rockies.*

Library of Congress ⊂℗ Data
Thybony, Scott.
   The Rockies : pillars of a continent / by Scott Thybony
   ;photographed by Paul Chesley.
      p.   cm.
   Includes index.
   ISBN 0-7922-2940-1. — ISBN 0-7922-2970-3 (deluxe ed.)
   1. Rocky Mountains—Description and travel.   I. Chesley, Paul,
1946-   .   II. Title.
   F721.T48   1996
   978—dc20   95-52391
                                                                   ⊂℗

Composition for this book by the National Geographic Society Book Division with the assistance of the Typographic section of National Geographic Production Services, Pre-Press Division. Printed and bound by R. R. Donelley & Sons, Willard, OH. Color separations by Digital Color Image, Pennsauken, NJ; Graphic Art Service, Inc., Nashville, TN; Penn Color Graphics, Inc., Huntingdon Valley, PA; and Phototype Color Graphics, Inc., Pennsauken, NJ. Dust jacket printed by Miken Systems, Inc., Cheektowaga, NY.